The World of Odysseus

M. I. FINLEY

NEW YORK

The Viking Press

1954

Library of Congress catalog card number: 54-9598

Printed in the U.S.A. by the Vail-Ballou Press

34709

To Mary

μάλιστα δέ τ' ἔκλυον αὐτοί

Contents

~~~~~~

Preface

BY MARK VAN DOREN

Readers of Homer have been rendered a service by Mr. Finley which can best be praised for the modesty and restraint of its rendering. It is an essential service, but Mr. Finley has nowhere claimed to do more than he promised: namely, to sketch the human society of which Homer conceived his heroes to be a part. It is necessary to know such things as this whenever we read stories about other days than our own; it is necessary, that is, to be made aware of motives and morals which differ, whether in kind or in degree, from those we assume to exist among our contemporaries. We can be overwhelmed, however, by one sort of scholar who undertakes the task, and who in the pride of his learning takes it for granted that without his aid we would not understand the story at all, or feel its force. Mr. Finley has the learning without the pride. He never makes the mistake of supposing that the greatest story-teller we have concerned himself with a set of motives and morals which only archaeology can reduce to comprehensible terms. He knows that if this had been true Homer would not have remained our greatest poet. He knows that Odysseus and Achilles were different from us in degree, not kind; that they both were and are strange men whom yet we can understand; that in fact there has always been that element of strangeness in them which we require in the heroes of stories—even contemporary stories— along with that other element of familiarity without which they would be monsters or chimeras. Mr. Finley has dealt with the strangeness in no such way as to dismiss or minimize the familiarity. His business is with the difference, and rightly, but he never doubts the sameness, which is where the greatness lies.

He reminds us that Homer, like Shakespeare after him, set his imagination free in a world that was earlier than his own yet by no means discontinuous with it. Shakespeare in his historical plays, whether English or Roman, reconstructed a vanished society which nevertheless was visible too—like as well as unlike the society of Elizabeth the Queen. A lesser poet would have confined himself to the unlikeness, and been forgotten fairly soon. But Falstaff is both far away and near at hand, as Richard II is, and Bolingbroke. Perhaps, as has been suggested, something of this sort must be true of any poet who hopes to keep his reputation; and it will be no less true when he handles contemporary types—the soldier, the detective, the politician, the lady of pleasure, or the lady indeed. Tolstoi's *War and Peace* goes back only one generation, or at the most two, to the Rostóvs and the Bolkónskis who in certain instances were the author's own ancestors. And what do they become in Tolstoi's hands? Both remote and recognizable, both romantic and real —figures in the round, and perhaps there is no other way to make them round.

But then there is the art of story-telling, an art whose rules have never changed. A right view of the past, or of the present either, or finally of both, is not in itself enough. Proportion, order, compassion, emphasis, and suspense—of these, no matter what his own time or the time of which he writes, the poet must be master. As Homer pre-eminently was; and Mr. Finley never obscures this paramount fact. It is astonishing how few stories have been told perfectly. Homer's were, for he knew how; and perhaps that is the first as well as the last thing to say about him. He is the best poet because he is the best artist. And we may be grateful to Mr. Finley because he nowhere assumes that we are ignorant of this, or that we as readers— normal, natural readers—are not the competent judges which of course we are. We are the only persons, that is to say, who know whether or not we are greatly interested as we read. So have many generations been before us, and so will our posterity be.

What Mr. Finley hopes to save us from is the consequence of expecting Homer's heroes to behave exactly as we think we might behave in similar circumstances, or might have behaved had we been there. There are certain things about Homer's world, Homer's special world, which he thinks we are entitled to know in order that we shall not charge Homer with being unjust, say, or merely odd. And he tells us these things with the greatest clarity and good sense. It was an aristocratic world, for example—like Shakespeare's, and like Tolstoi's in *War and Peace* (though not of course in the later tales of artisans and peasants). It was a world with unique views of hospitality; it was a world whose gods were more like men than gods have ever been before or since. It was a world exclusively, or almost exclusively, of warriors and kings, a world where few things counted except riches, prowess, and honor. It was a world primarily of men, not of women and children. It was a world of war, with slaves and captives in it as well as chieftains and the heads of households. These things Mr. Finley makes excellently clear; and then he leaves us with a poet who, so conditioned and circumscribed, proceeded to give us master-pieces in which our own imaginations may feel at home. That is the final wonder, as the Greeks knew within a century after Homer's death, and as all readers since have known, whatever the century or society in which they happened to be born.

THE WORLD OF ODYSSEUS

CHAPTER I

Homer and the Greeks

"By the general consent of criticks," wrote Dr. Johnson, "the first praise of genius is due to the writer of an epick poem, as it requires an assemblage of all the powers which are singly sufficient for other compositions." He was thinking of John Milton then, and he concluded his life of the English poet with these words: "His work is not the greatest of heroick poems, only because it is not the first." That title had been pre-empted for all time by Homer, whom the Greeks called simply "the poet."

No other poet, no other literary figure in all history, for that matter, occupied a place in the life of his people such as Homer's. He was their pre-eminent symbol of nationhood, the unimpeachable authority on their earliest history, and a decisive figure in the creation of their pantheon, as well as their most beloved and most widely quoted poet. Plato tells us that there were Greeks who firmly believed that Homer "educated Hellas and that he deserves to be taken up as an instructor in the management and culture of human affairs, and that a man ought to regulate the whole of his life by following this poet." [1] * Faced with such a judgment, on first looking into the *Iliad* or *Odyssey*

* References to numbers may be found under "Source References" at the back of the book.

3

one anticipates a Bible or some great treatise in philosophy, only to find two long narrative poems, one devoted to a few days in the ten-year war between Greeks and Trojans, the other to the homecoming troubles of Odysseus (whom the Romans knew as Ulysses).

Homer was a man's name, not the Greek equivalent of "Anonymous," and that is the one certain fact about him. Who he was, where he lived, when he composed, these are questions we cannot answer with assurance, any more than could the Greeks themselves. In truth, it is probable that the *Iliad* and the *Odyssey* which we read were the works of two men, not of one. They stand at the beginning of extant Greek literature— and hence of European letters—along with the writings of Hesiod, who lived in central Greece in the district called Boeotia. Modern students think that the *Iliad* surely and the *Odyssey* probably were not composed on the Greek mainland but on one of the islands in the Aegean Sea or still farther east on the peninsula of Asia Minor (now Turkey). And they think that the period between 750 and 650 B.C. was the century of this earliest literature.

For the long history of the Greeks before the time of Homer and Hesiod there is only the mute testimony of the stones, the pottery, and the metal objects unearthed by archaeologists. Intricate analysis of the remains and of place names has demonstrated that people speaking the Greek language, but ignorant of the art of writing, first appeared on the scene about 2000 B.C. Where they came from originally no one knows. In Plato's day, some fifteen hundred years later, they were to be found scattered over a tremendous territory from Trebizond near the eastern end of the Black Sea to the Mediterranean shores of France and North Africa—perhaps five or six million souls all

told. These migrants were not the first inhabitants of Greece by
any means, nor did they come as highly civilized conquerors
overwhelming savage tribes. Archaeologists have discovered
ample evidence of relatively advanced pre-Greek civilizations,
some traced back well into the Stone Age, before 3000 B.C. By
and large, the level of social and material development in the
area was much superior to that of the newcomers. When the
people whose language was Greek arrived, they came not in one
mass migration, not as a sweeping destructive horde, not in a
great trek across the difficult mountain terrain of northern
Greece, not as an organized colonizing expedition, but rather
in a process of infiltration lasting nearly a thousand years.

The human mind plays strange tricks with time perspectives
when the distant past is under consideration: centuries become
as years and millennia as decades. It requires conscious effort
to make the necessary correction, to appreciate that an infiltration over several centuries would not appear to the participants
as a single connected movement at all; that, in other words,
neither the Greeks nor the natives into whose world they came
were likely to have any idea that something big and historic
was taking place. Instead they saw individual occurrences,
sometimes peaceable and in no way noteworthy, sometimes
troublesome and even violently destructive of lives and ways
of life. Biologically and culturally these were centuries of thor-
ough intermixture. There is a clear reminiscence of the situation in the *Odyssey,* when Odysseus says, jumbling Greek and
aboriginal names together: "There is a land called Crete in the
midst of the wine-dark sea . . . and in it are many men beyond number and ninety cities. And there is a mixture of
tongues; there are Achaeans there, and great-hearted Eteo-
Cretans, and Cydonians and Dorians of the waving hair and

illustrious Pelasgians." [2] Skeletal remains show the biological fusion; language and religion provide the chief evidence with respect to culture. The end product, after a thousand years or so, was the historical people we call the Greeks. In a significant sense, the original migrants were not Greeks, but people who spoke Greek and who were to become one element in a later composite which could lay proper claim to the name. The Angles and Saxons in Britain offer a convenient analogy: they were not Englishmen, but they were to become Englishmen one day.

It was to take the Greeks more than a thousand years to acquire a name of their own—and today they have two. In their own language they are Hellenes, and their country is Hellas. *Graeci* is the name given to them by the Romans and later adopted generally in Europe. In antiquity, furthermore, their eastern neighbors used still a third name for them—Ionians, the Iavones of the Old Testament. And all three are late, for we find none of them in Homer. He called his people Argives, Danaans, and, most frequently, Achaeans. Now Achaeans, it so happens, appear quite early in non-Greek sources. In the great Hittite archive discovered at Boghaz-Keui in North Central Turkey there are several references in the period 1365–1200 B.C. to a kingdom called in Hittite Achchiyava, one of whose rulers was named Atarshiyash. On linguistic grounds, it is reasonable to identify Achchiyava with Achaea, and perhaps Atarshiyash with Atreus, in the Homeric poems the father of Agamemnon, the Greek commander-in-chief, and of Menelaus, king of the Spartans and husband of Helen of Troy. Achchiyava cannot be located with any certainty, but the probability is that it was either the island of Rhodes or some place on the

Greek mainland. But wherever it was, it was only a local kingdom within the total Greek area, and nothing more.

It is idle to speculate when the word Achaean came to be
applied to all Greeks, or why. In 1350 B.C. it was surely not.
Near the end of the following century we meet the Achaeans
again, this time as participants with other peoples in a great
but unsuccessful sea raid on Egypt. The victorious monarch,
the Pharaoh Merneptah, had the list of his captives and trophies
inscribed on the walls of the temple at Karnak on the Nile. One
entry refers to the Achaeans, "whose hands were carried off,
for they had no foreskins." [3] Circumcision was a common
enough practice in the eastern Mediterranean but it was absolutely unknown among the Greeks in historical times. The people of Achchiyava who were powerful enough to raid Egypt
and Hittite territory were evidently still in the formative stage
of becoming Greeks, still non-Greek as well as Greek. When
the local name "Achaean" became the word for all the Greeks,
even if not the exclusive word and even if only for a brief period
before it was replaced by "Hellene," the formative period may
be considered ended: the common name is a symbol that Greek
history proper had been launched.* For us, that means with the
Iliad.

It goes without saying that the formation of a Greek people
and a Greek civilization was not a planned process or in any
narrow sense a conscious one. Trial and error and imitation
were the chief techniques, so that a measure of social and cul-
tural diversity, often of the most striking kind, was characteristic of Hellas in its infancy. Indeed the tempo and direction
of change continued to vary throughout Greek history.

* After Homer, both Achaea and Argos survived as local place names,
districts in southern Greece.

One element, however, was remarkably stable all the time. The language with which the migrants entered Greece is classified as a member of the numerous Indo-European family, which includes the ancient languages of India (Sanskrit) and Persia, Armenian, the Slavic tongues, several Baltic languages (Lithuanian, for instance), Albanian, the Italic languages, among which are Latin and its modern descendants, the Celtic group, of which Gaelic and Welsh have retained some vitality to our own day, the Germanic languages, and various dead languages once spoken in the Mediterranean region, like Hittite (now recovered), Phrygian, and Illyrian.

For a very long time, until about 300 B.C., Greek was a language of many dialects. But the differences among them were chiefly in matters of pronunciation and spelling, less frequently in vocabulary and syntax. They were considerable, but still not so great as to render a speaker in one dialect utterly unintelligible to men brought up on another, perhaps no more so than in the extreme modern instance of a Neapolitan coming to Venice. Even the artificial poetic dialect of Homer, with its Aeolic base embedded in an Ionian frame and its many coined words and forms made necessary by the meter, was apparently understood well enough by the uneducated as well as the learned all over the Greek world.

Exactly when the Greeks began to write has been a secret locked in the undeciphered tablets of Crete and Mycenae; the most recent investigations suggest the date may go back as far as 1400 B.C. The decisive point, however, came considerably later, when the Greeks took over the so-called Phoenician alphabet. With the signs came the Phoenician names for the letters, so that perfectly good Semitic words—*aleph,* an ox; *bet,* a house—were turned into Greek nonsense syllables, *alpha, beta,* and so on. The actual borrowing process can be neither described nor dated very closely: the guesses range between 1000 and 750 B.C. The one thing that is certain about the operation is its deliberate, rational character, for whoever was responsible did much more than imitate. The Phoenician sign system was not simply copied; it was modified radically to fit the needs of the Greek language, which is totally unrelated to the Semitic family.

Equipped with this remarkable new invention, the Greeks could now record everything imaginable, from the owner's name scratched on a clay jug to a book-length poem like the *Iliad*. But what they wrote down and what remains today are utterly disproportionate in their bulk. Ancient literature, broadly understood to include science, philosophy, and social analysis, as well as belles-lettres, faced a severe struggle for survival. The works of Homer and Plato and Euclid were written by hand on scrolls, usually of the papyrus reed. From the originals, copies were made, always by hand, on papyrus or later on parchment (vellum). None of these materials is everlasting. What survived was, apart from some accidental exceptions, what was deemed worthy of being copied and recopied for hundreds of years of Greek history and then through more hundreds of years of Byzantine history, centuries in which values and fashions changed more than once, often radically.

How little came through this sifting process is easily illustrated. The names of some 150 Greek authors of tragedy are known, but, apart from odd scraps quoted by later Greek or Roman authors and anthologists, the plays of only 3, Athenians of the fifth century B.C., are extant. Nor is that the end of it. Aeschylus wrote 82 plays, and we have 7 in full; Sophocles is said to have written 123, of which 7 still exist; and we can read 19 of Euripides' 92. What we read, furthermore, if we read the Greek original, is a text laboriously collated from medieval manuscripts, usually from the twelfth to the fifteenth centuries of our era, the end product of an unknown number of recopyings, and therefore always of possibly distorted transcription.

Only in Egypt was it possible for written papyrus texts to last indefinitely, thanks to the natural dehydration provided by the peculiar climatic conditions. Egypt came under Greek control in the empire of Alexander the Great, after which there was extensive migration of Greeks to the Nile. From the third century B.C. to the Arab conquest a thousand years later, Greek was the language of letters in Egypt, and many of the papyrus finds contain literary fragments that are much older than the medieval manuscripts. In a few cases—the works of the lyric poet Bacchylides, some comedies of Menander, the mimes of Herondas, Aristotle's little book on the Athenian constitution —the papyri have even brought back to light notable works that had been altogether lost. Their number is so small, however, as to underscore the fact that the process of elimination had been under way long before the monkish copyists of medieval Christendom. In the library established at Alexandria by the Greek rulers of Egypt in the third century before Christ, the greatest library of the ancient world, only 74 or 78 of Euripides' 92 plays were available, revealing a considerable loss in the relatively short span of two centuries. At Alexandria and elsewhere scholars and librarians then resisted the process of desuetude, preserving many works in which general interest had declined or died out altogether. But in the early centuries of the Christian era there was an end even to such efforts, and the disappearance of ancient books proceeded rapidly.

The papyri of Egypt also make it abundantly clear that, in

the struggle for literary survival, Homer was without a rival. Of all the scraps and fragments of literary works found in Egypt that had been published by 1949, there is a total of 1233 books by authors whose names are identifiable. This figure represents individual copies, not separate titles. Of the 1233, nearly one-half—555, to be precise—were copies of the *Iliad* or *Odyssey,* or commentaries upon them. The *Iliad* outnumbered the *Odyssey* by 380 to 113. The next most "popular" author was the orator Demosthenes, with 74 papyri (again including commentaries), followed by Euripides with 54 and Hesiod with 40. Plato is represented by but 36 papyri, Aristotle by 6. These are figures of book-copying among the Greeks in Egypt after Alexander, to be sure, but all the evidence indicates that they may be taken as fairly typical of the Greek world generally. If a Greek owned any books—that is, papyrus rolls—he was almost as likely to own the *Iliad* and *Odyssey* as anything from the rest of Greek literature.

There were thinkers among the Greeks who doubted that this was good or desirable. To those who called Homer the teacher of Hellas, Plato replied: Yes, he is "first and most poetical among the tragic poets," but a proper society would bar all poetry "with the sole exception of hymns to the gods and encomia to the good." [4] Two centuries earlier the philosopher Xenophanes had protested that "Homer and Hesiod have attributed to the gods everything that is disgraceful and blameworthy among men: theft, adultery, and deceit." [5] Like Plato, he recognized the tremendous hold Homer had on the Greeks, and he thought that the effect was all bad.

Homer, it is essential to recall, was not just a poet; he was a teller of myths and legends. The mythmaking process had of course begun among the Greeks many centuries earlier, and it went on continuously wherever there were Greeks, always by word of mouth and always ceremonially. It was activity on the highest social level, not just the casual daydreaming of a poet here, a more imaginative peasant there. The essential subject matter of myth was action, not ideas, creeds, or symbolic representations, but happenings, occurrences—wars, floods, adventures by land, sea, and air, family quarrels, births, marriages, and deaths. As men listened to the narratives, in rituals, at ceremonial games, or on other social occasions, they lived through a vicarious experience. They believed the narrative implicitly. "In mythical imagination there is always implied an act of *belief*. Without the belief in the reality of its object, myth would lose its ground." [6]

That may be true of savages, one may object at this point, but the Greeks were not savages. They were too civilized to believe that it was the god Poseidon who bodily prevented Odysseus from reaching his home in Ithaca, or that Zeus impregnated Leda in the guise of a swan, or that there were witches like Circe with the power to turn men into swine. These are symbolic tales, allegories, parables, perhaps dreamlike reflections of the unconscious, conveying elaborate ethical and psychological analyses and insights.

Nothing could be more wrong. Where he is able to study "myth which is still alive" and not "mummified," not "enshrined in the indestructible but lifeless repository of dead religions," the anthropologist discovers that myth "is not of the nature of fiction . . . but it is a living reality, believed to have once happened." [7] The Greeks of Homer were not primitive men, like Malinowski's Trobrianders; they lived in what is often called, by convention, an archaic society. And the Greeks of the succeeding centuries were remarkably civilized people. Yet the bitterness of Xenophanes in the sixth century B.C. and of Plato in the fourth proves precisely that, with respect to myth, many of their fellow citizens shared the Trobriander view, or at least were closer to it than to the symbolist view. Plato himself had no doubts about the veracity of the *history* in Homer; it was the philosophy and morality that he rejected, the notions of justice and the gods, of good and evil, not the tale of Troy.

We must not underestimate the intellectual feat that it was for later generations to separate out the strands of the Homeric tales, to recreate the Trojan War without the arrows of Apollo or the *Odyssey* without the gale-producing breath of Poseidon. Few Greeks ever attained the outright rejection of the traditional myth found in Xenophanes. Between that extreme and the primitive acceptance in full there were many intermediate points, and Greeks could be found at each. Writing toward the end of the fifth century B.C., the historian Herodotus said, "The Hellenes tell many things without proper examination; among them is the silly myth they tell about Heracles." That myth describes how Heracles (now better known in the Latin form, Hercules) went to Egypt, was about to be sacrificed to Zeus, and at the last moment slew all his captors. How silly, says Herodotus, when a study of Egyptian customs reveals that human sacrifice was unthinkable among them.[8] But Herodotus had no difficulty in believing that Heracles actually existed once upon a time. In fact, he thought there had been two. Herodotus was a widely traveled man; he found what he identified as Heracles myths and Heracles cults, or parallels, everywhere, in Phoenician Tyre and in Egypt as well as among Hellenes. He tried to sift out truth from fable and to reconcile contradictions and discrepancies. Among the conclusions to which he came were that the name Heracles was originally Egyptian—for

which Plutarch later accused him of being a "barbarian-lover"
—and that there were actually two figures of that name, one a
god, the other a hero.

What else could Herodotus have done? The accumulated
tradition of centuries of myths and legends, sacred and profane,
was all there was in the way of early Greek history. Some of it
was obviously self-contradictory from the beginning. In one
respect the ancient Greeks were always a divided people. They
entered the Mediterranean world in small groups, and even
when they settled and finally took control they remained dis-
united in their political organization. By Herodotus's time, and
for many years before, Greek settlements were to be found not
only all over the area of modern Hellas but also along the Black
Sea, on the shores of what is now Turkey, in southern Italy and
eastern Sicily, on the North African coast, and on the littoral
of southern France. Within this ellipse of some fifteen hundred
miles at the poles, there were hundreds and hundreds of communities, often differing in their political structures and always
insisting on their separate sovereignties. Neither then nor at
any time in the ancient world was there a nation, a single national territory under one sovereign rule, called Greece (or any
synonym for Greece).

Such a world could not possibly have produced a unified,
consistent national mythology. In the early centuries, when
myth-creation was an active process in its most vital and living
stage, the myths necessarily underwent constant alteration.
Each new tribe, each new community, each shift in power relations within the aristocratic elite, meant some change in the
genealogies of heroes, in the outcome of past family feuds, in
the delicate balances among men and gods. Obviously the new

version developed in one area did not coincide with the old, or new, versions known in dozens of other areas. Nor was agreement sought. Neither the myth-tellers nor their audiences were scholars; they were participants in their own social activities and they were not in the least concerned with the myths of others. It was altogether another world when a historian like Herodotus engaged in the study of comparative mythology. Then it became necessary to manipulate the traditional accounts —manipulate, but not discard. They were checked for inner consistency, corrected and amplified with the knowledge acquired from the very much older records and traditions of other peoples—Egyptians and Babylonians, in particular—and rationalized wherever possible. Thus purified, they could be retained, as history if not as anything more.

A human society without myth has never been known, and indeed it is doubtful whether such a society is at all possible. One measure of man's advance from his most primitive beginnings to something we call civilization is the way in which he controls his myths, his ability to distinguish between the areas of behavior, the extent to which he can bring more and more of his activity under the rule of reason. In that advance the Greeks have been pre-eminent. Perhaps their greatest achievement lay in their discovery—more precisely, in Socrates' discovery—that man is "that being who, when asked a rational question, can give a rational answer." [9] Homer was so far from Socrates that he was not even cognizant of man as an integrated psychic whole. Nevertheless, Homer occupies the first stage in the history of Greek control over its myths; his poems are often pre-Greek, as it were, in their treatment of myth, but they also have flashes of something else, of a genius for ordering the world, for bringing man and nature, men and the gods, into harmony in a way that succeeding centuries were to expand and elevate to the glory of Hellenism.

If it is true that European history began with the Greeks, it is equally true that Greek history began with the world of Odysseus. And, like all human beginnings, it had a long history behind it. For history, as Jacob Burckhardt remarked, is the one field of study in which one cannot begin at the beginning.

CHAPTER II

Bards and Heroes

The tale of man's decline and fall has been told in many ways. One elaborately patterned version, probably Iranian in origin, had man destined to pass through four ages, four steps taking him farther and farther from justice and morality, from the paradise in which the gods had originally placed him. Each age was symbolized by a metal: in descending order, gold, silver, bronze or copper, and iron.

In due course this myth traveled west to Greece. But when first we meet it there, in the *Works and Days* of Hesiod, it has acquired an altogether new element. Between the age of bronze and the iron age of the present, a fifth has intruded.

"But when the earth had covered this (bronze) generation also, Zeus the son of Cronus made yet another, the fourth, upon the fruitful earth, which was nobler and more righteous, a god-like race of hero-men who are called demi-gods, the race before our own, throughout the boundless earth. Grim war and dread battle destroyed a part of them, some in the land of Cadmus at seven-gated Thebes when they fought for the flocks of Oedipus, and some, when it had brought them in ships over the great sea gulf to Troy for rich-haired Helen's sake: there death's end en-

shrouded a part of them. But to the others father Zeus the son
of Cronus gave a living and an abode apart from men, and made
them dwell at the ends of earth. And they lived untouched
by sorrow in the islands of the blessed along the shore of deep
swirling Ocean, happy heroes for whom the grain-giving earth
bears honey-sweet fruit flourishing thrice a year. . . ." [1]

We do not know whether it was Hesiod or some nameless
predecessor who converted the eastern myth of four ages into
this Hellenic myth of five ages. Nor does it matter, for the substance is clear. A separate Greek tradition was imposed on the
ill-digested importation, and the fusion was loosely and care-
lessly accomplished. By the time the eastern myth came to
Greece the Hellenes had firmly fixed in their past history an age
of heroes. Under no circumstances would they surrender that
brief period of honor and glory. Instead they inserted it into
the sequence of metals, leaving it to modern scholars to dig out
the crudities and the contradictions and to piece out explanations.

That there had once been a time of heroes few Greeks, early
or late, ever doubted. They knew all about them: their names,
their genealogies, and their exploits. Homer was their most
authoritative source of information, but by no means the only
one. Unfortunately, neither Homer nor Hesiod had the slightest
interest in history as we might understand the notion. The poets'
concern was with certain facts of the past, not with their relationship to other facts, past or present, and, in the case of Homer, not even with the consequences of those facts. The outcome
of the Trojan War, the fall and destruction of Troy and the fruits
of Greek victory, would have been of prime importance to a
historian of the war. Yet the poet of the *Iliad* was utterly in-

different to all that, the poet of the *Odyssey* scarcely less so. Similarly with the ages of man. In the Zoroastrian version there is a mathematical precision: each age was of 3000 years, and in each law and morality declined by one-fourth. In Hesiod there is not even a whisper about date or duration, just as Homer gives no indication of the date of the Trojan War other than "once upon a time."

Later Greeks worked the chronology out in detail. Although they did not reach entire agreement, few departed very far from a date equivalent to 1200 B.C. for the war with Troy and a period of four generations as the age of the heroes. Homer, they decided, lived four hundred years later, and Hesiod was his contemporary—in one tradition, even his cousin.

Heroes are ubiquitous, of course. There are always men called heroes; and that is misleading, for the identity of label conceals a staggering diversity of substance. In a sense, they always seek honor and glory, and that too may be misleading without further definition of the contents of honor and the road to glory. Few of the heroes of history, or of literature from the Athenian drama of the fifth century B.C. to our own time, shared the singlemindedness of their Homeric counterparts. For the latter everything pivoted on a single element of honor and virtue: strength, bravery, physical courage, prowess. Conversely, there was no weakness, no unheroic trait, but one, and that was cowardice and the consequent failure to pursue heroic goals.

"O Zeus and the other gods," prayed Hector, "grant that this my son shall become as I am, most distinguished among the Trojans, as strong and valiant, and that he rule by might in Ilion. And then may men say, 'He is far braver than his father,' as he returns from war. May he bring back spoils stained with the blood of men he has slain, and may his mother's heart rejoice." * There is no social conscience in these words, no trace of the Decalogue, no responsibility other than familial, no obligation to anyone or anything but one's own prowess and one's own drive to victory and power.

The age of heroes, then, as Homer understood it, was a time in which men exceeded subsequent standards with respect to a specified and severely limited group of qualities. In a measure, these virtues, these values and capacities, were shared by many men of the period, for otherwise there could have been no distinct age of heroes between the bronze and the iron. Particularly in the *Odyssey* the word "hero" is a class term for the whole aristocracy, and at times it even seems to embrace all the free men. "Tomorrow," Athena instructed Telemachus, "summon the Achaean heroes to an assembly," [2] by which she meant "call the regular assembly of Ithaca."

That in fact there had never been a four-generation heroic age in Greece, in the precise, self-contained sense of Homer, scarcely requires demonstration. The serious problem for the historian is to determine whether, and to what extent, there is anything in the poems that relates to social and historical reality; how much, in other words, of the world of Odysseus existed only in the poet's head and how much outside, in space and time. The prior question to be considered is whence the poet took his ideas about that world and his stories of its wars and its heroes' private lives.

---

* *Iliad* 6.476–81. A problem of translation may be noted here. In Homeric psychology, every feeling, emotion, or idea was attributed to an organ of the body, such as the heart or the unidentifiable *thymos*. Sometimes the feeling itself was given the name of the organ. Such phrases are scarcely translatable. I have usually rendered all these words by "heart," to fit our customary metaphorical usage, although the sense in Homer is much more literal.

The heroic poem, a genre of which the *Iliad* and *Odyssey* are the greatest examples, must be distinguished from the literary epic like the *Aeneid* or *Paradise Lost*. Heroic poetry is always oral poetry; it is composed orally, often by bards who are illiterate, and it is recited in a chant to a listening audience. Formally, it is at once distinguishable by the constant repetition of phrases, lines, and whole groups of lines. The coming of day is nearly always, in Homer, "And when rosy-fingered Dawn appeared, the child of morn." When a verbal message is sent (and Homeric messages are never in writing), the poet has the messenger hear the exact text and then repeat it to the recipient word for word. Athena is "owl-eyed," the island of Ithaca "sea-girt," Achilles "city-sacking." Yet this is no simple, monotonous repetition. There are thirty-six different epithets for Achilles, for example, and the choice is rigorously determined by the position in the line and the required syntactical form. It has been calculated that there are some twenty-five formulaic expressions, or fragments of formulas, in the first twenty-five lines of the *Iliad* alone. About one-third of the entire poem consists of lines or blocks of lines which occur more than once in the work, and the same is true of the *Odyssey*.

Sophisticated readers of printed books have often misunderstood the device of repetition as a mark of limited imagination and of the primitive state of the art of poetry. Thus French critics of the sixteenth and seventeenth centuries placed Vergil above Homer precisely because the former did not repeat himself but always found a new phrasing and new combinations. What they failed to perceive was that the repeated formula is indispensable in heroic poetry. The bard composes directly before his audience; he does not recite memorized lines. In 1934, at the request of Professor Milman Parry, a sixty-year-old Serbian bard who could neither read nor write recited for him a poem of the length of the *Odyssey,* making it up as he went along, yet retaining meter and form and building a complicated narrative. The performance took two weeks, with a week in between, the bard chanting for two hours each morning and two more in the afternoon.

Such a feat makes enormous demands in concentration on both the bard and his audience. That it can be done at all is attributable to the fact that the poet, a professional with long years of apprenticeship behind him, has at his disposal the necessary raw materials: masses of incidents and masses of formulas, the accumulation of generations of minstrels who came before him. The Greek stock included the many varied and hopelessly contradictory myths that had been created in connection with their religious rites; all kinds of tales about mortal heroes, some fanciful and some reasonably accurate; and the formulas that could fit any incident: the coming of dawn and of the night, scenes of combat and burial and feasting, the ordinary activities of men—arising and eating and drinking and dreaming—descriptions of palaces and meadows, arms and treasure, metaphors of the sea or of pasturage, and so on beyond enumeration. Out of these building blocks the poet constructs his work, and each work—each performance, in other words—is a new one, though all the elements may be old and well known.

Repetition of the familiar is equally essential for the audience. To follow a long and many-faceted tale, often told over many days and nights, chanted in a language that is not the language of everyday speech, with its metrically imposed artificial word order and its strange grammatical forms and vocabulary, is also no mean achievement, made possible by precisely the same formulaic devices that are indispensable for the creator. Poet and audience alike rest frequently, so to speak, as the familiar rosy-fingered Dawns and the messages repeated word for word roll forth. While they rest, the one prepares the next line or episode, the others prepare to attend to it.

Now it is possible, as has recently been argued, that the *Iliad* as we know it was composed in writing, and not orally. And it is nearly indisputable that the *Iliad* has a quality of originality and genius beyond all other heroic poems, even the best of them—*Beowulf,* for instance, or *The Cid* or *The Song of Roland.* Even so, both the *Iliad* and the *Odyssey* reveal in fullest measure all the essential characteristics of unwritten heroic poetry the world over. Behind them lay long practice in the art of the bard, which had evolved the remarkable but totally artificial dialect of the poems, a dialect which no Greek ever spoke but which remained permanently fixed as the language of Greek epic. Behind them, too, lay the generations that had created the formulaic elements, the building blocks of the poems.

With the *Iliad* and the *Odyssey* Greek heroic poetry reached its glory. Soon the bard who composed as he chanted began to give way to the rhapsodist who was primarily a reciter of memorized lines, and to the hack who prepared rehashed versions with scant literary merit. New forms composed in writing, the short lyric and then the drama, replaced the oral epic as the vehicles of artistic expression. Just when the shift occurred is disputed by the experts without end, and without a semblance of agreement. One plausible view is that the *Iliad* took roughly, but not precisely, the form in which we now have it in the eighth century before Christ, more likely in the latter

half of the century than in the earlier; that Hesiod flourished a
generation or so later; and that the *Odyssey* was composed still
another generation or two after Hesiod.

Such a dating scheme, with two Homers a hundred years
apart, seems at first thought to be impossible. For more than
two thousand years men of taste, intelligence, and expert knowledge never questioned the tradition that one man wrote both
the *Iliad* and the *Odyssey,* and their unanimous judgment had
the support of the style and language of the poems, which are
virtually indistinguishable. But once the technique of ancient
bardic composition was rediscovered, and with it the secret of
the deceptive uniformity of style, then the really great differences
between the two poems could be seen in their full perspective.
Some of these differences had already drawn comment in antiquity. The Roman Pliny noted that there is more magic in the
Odyssey, and he was right to a degree. In the *Iliad* the interventions of the gods have the character of minor miracles, but
not even Achilles possess magical powers, though his divine
mother Thetis watches over him constantly. The *Odyssey* has
similar interventions, but it also has the Circe episode, which
rests on a series of magical formulas in the most precise sense
and form.

A more striking distinction is to be observed in the relations
between the heroes and the gods. Although the basic decisions
are made on Olympus in both tales, in the *Iliad* the gods interfere spasmodically, in the *Odyssey* Athena leads Odysseus and
Telemachus step by step. The later poem opens in heaven with
Athena's appeal to Zeus to bring the hero's trials to an end,
and it closes when the goddess puts a stop to the blood feud between the hero and the kinsmen of the suitors he had killed.
Even the motivation of the gods differs; in the *Iliad* it is per-

sonal, the expression of the likes and dislikes of individual deities for one hero or another, whereas in the *Odyssey* the personal element has been supplemented, in part and in still rudimentary fashion, by the requirements of justice.

The *Iliad* is filled with the action of heroes. Even when it departs from its central theme, the wrath of Achilles, its attention never wavers from heroic deeds and interests. The *Odyssey*, although shorter, has two distinct and essentially unconnected themes: the fairy-tale wanderings of Odysseus and the struggle for power in Ithaca. Given its location in an age of heroes, the *Odyssey* has only one proper hero, Odysseus himself. His companions are faceless mediocrities. His son Telemachus is sweet and dutiful, and when he grows up he may develop into a hero, but the poet does not take him that far. The suitors for Penelope's hand are villains—an incongruity, because "hero" and "villain" are not yet proper antonyms; they are not even commensurable terms; hence there are no villains in the *Iliad*. Penelope herself is little more than a convenient "mythologically available character." [3] Penelope became a moral heroine for later generations, the embodiment of goodness and chastity, to be contrasted with the faithless, murdering Clytaemnestra, Agamemnon's wife; but "hero" has no feminine gender in the age of heroes.

Finally, the *Iliad* is oriented eastward, from the vantage point of Greece, the *Odyssey* to the west. Greek relations with the west began relatively late, not before the middle of the eighth century B.C., in rather tentative fashion, to become, in the following century, extensive penetration and migration into Sicily, southern Italy, and beyond. The presumption is, then, that the *Odyssey* reflects this new aspect of Greek history by taking traditional materials and facing them westward. This is not to say that the travels of Odysseus in Never-Never Land can be retraced on a map. All attempts to do just that, and they have been numerous from ancient times on, have foundered. Even the topographical detail of Odysseus' home island of Ithaca can be shown to be a jumble, with several essential points appropriate to the neighboring isle of Leucas but quite impossible for Ithaca.

Despite these differences, however, the *Iliad* and *Odyssey* stand together as against the poems of Hesiod, particularly his *Works and Days*. For all his use of the language and the formulas, Hesiod does not properly belong with the heroic poets. Whenever he treats of matters that are not obvious myth, when he deals with human society and human behavior, he is always personal and contemporary in his outlook. Neither heroes nor ordinary mortals of a past age are his characters, but Hesiod himself, his brother, his neighbors. Hesiod is wholly a part of the iron age of the present, specifically of the archaic Greek world of the eighth and seventh centuries B.C.

Not so the *Iliad* or *Odyssey*. They look to a departed era, and their substance is unmistakably old. The *Odyssey* in particular encompasses a wide field of human activities and relationships: social structure and family life, royalty, aristocrats, and commoners, banqueting and plowing and swineherding. These are things about which we know a little as regards the seventh century, in which the *Odyssey* was apparently composed, and what we know and what the *Odyssey* relates are simply not the same. It is enough to point to the *polis* (city-state) form of political organization, widespread in the Hellenic world by then. On the island of Chios, which made the strongest claim to being "Homer's" birthplace, the *polis* had even moved to democracy, on the evidence of a fragmentary stone inscription scarcely later in date than the *Odyssey*. Yet neither poem has any trace of a *polis* in its classical political sense. *Polis* in Homer means nothing more than a fortified site, a town. The poets of the *Iliad* and *Odyssey*, unlike Hesiod, were basically neither personal nor contemporary in their reference.

In our present texts, each poem is divided into twenty-four "books," one for each letter of the Greek alphabet. This was a late arrangement, the work of the Alexandrian scholars, and its arbitrariness is apparent. The individual books vary in length and they do not always have unity of content, although many are so self-contained that one is tempted to think of them as having been planned for recitation at a single sitting. Properly to dissect the poems, one must read them without reference to the Alexandrian division. Then it becomes clear how in the *Odyssey* the story of the Trojan War, the struggle with the suitors, and a fairy tale, the adventures of a Greek Sinbad the Sailor, were all stitched together—a rhapsodist was literally a "stitcher of songs"—along with many little pieces, like the myth of the adultery between Ares and Aphrodite, myths of the afterlife, or the account of the kidnaping of a young prince and his sale into slavery (the swineherd Eumaeus). The *Iliad* may not have as obviously independent large pieces, but the snippets are innumerable. Each reminiscence and genealogical tale could have circulated, and unquestionably did, as an independent short heroic poem. The account of the funeral games for Patroclus was appropriate, with no more alteration than a change in the names, whenever the narrative required the burial of a hero. The bits of Olympian mythology fit anywhere.

The genius of the *Iliad* and *Odyssey* does not lie in the individual pieces, or even in the language, for that was all a common stock of materials available to any bard in excessive quantity. The pre-eminence of a Homer lies in the scale on which he worked and in the freshness with which he selected and manipulated what he inherited, in the little variations and inventions he introduced—in the stitching. Paradoxically, the greater the mass of accumulated materials, the greater the poet's freedom, given a desire and the ability to exercise it. Through his unparalleled skill in choice of incidents and background formulas and in his combinations, a Homer could create a world in his own image, strikingly different in certain essentials from what older bards had passed on to him, and yet, in appearance, remain within the fixed path of bardic tradition, and, in fact, retain a large part of that traditional world.

Merely as narrative, the *Iliad* and *Odyssey* together, for all their unprecedented length, omit very much of what was in their time the accepted history of the Trojan War and its aftermath. This was a matter of free decision, for the poets knew the whole history well, as they assumed their audiences did too. Then other long, clearly inferior epics were composed from the traditional stock, until there was a cycle of seven poems, telling the story from the creation of the gods to the death of Odysseus and the marriage of Telemachus and Circe. For a time they were all attributed to Homer; the Homer whom Xenophanes attacked was probably a collective name for the Trojan cycle.* However, the incomparable qualities of the *Iliad* and *Odyssey* were early apparent, although not until the fourth and third centuries B.C. was it concluded that Homer did not write the rest of the cycle as well. The other poems survived for five or six hundred years thereafter and then they

---

* Xenophanes was born about 570 B.C., perhaps no more than two generations after the composition of the *Odyssey*. The sharpness of his critique thus testifies to both the enormous popular appeal of the poems and the rapidity of their acceptance.

disappeared, except for a few verses in anthologies or quotations.

Conceivably the bards who finally shaped the *Iliad* and *Odyssey* did so in writing. However, the diffusion of the two poems was oral. The Greek world of the eighth and seventh centuries B.C. was deeply unlettered, despite the introduction of the alphabet. In fact, Greek literature continued to be oral for a very long time. The tragedies, for example, were surely composed in writing; but they were read by men who could be counted perhaps in the hundreds, and they were heard and reheard by many tens of thousands all over Hellas. The recitation of poetry, heroic, lyric, or dramatic, was always an essential feature of the numerous religious festivals. The origins of that practice are lost in the prehistoric era, when myth was often ritual drama, the vivid re-enactment before the assembled people of the procession of the seasons or whatever other phenomenon inspired the ceremony. In historical times ritual drama lived on and continued to flourish in the Demeter cult and other rites known collectively as "mysteries." But they were no longer the great festive occasions of dramatic performance and poetic recitation. Homer's place was in the official celebrations honoring the Olympic gods, some pan-Hellenic, like the quadrennial Olympic games dedicated to Zeus, others pan-Ionian, like the festival of the Delian Apollo, still others purely local, like the annual Panathenaic in Athens. There ritual drama was gone, except for vestigial remains; instead, the gods were celebrated by other means, which invoked a less direct and less "primitive" communion between men and the immortals.

In large part the reciters and performers were professionals, and it is one of the interesting facts of social history that in

many sectors of the world they were among the first to break
the primeval rule that a man lives, works, and dies within his
tribe or community. There is a hint of this in the *Odyssey* when
the swineherd Eumaeus, berated for having brought a foreign
beggar to the banquet in the palace, disingenuously countered
the charge with a rhetorical question: "For who ever summons
a stranger from abroad and brings him along, unless he be one
of the craftsmen (*demioergoi*), a seer or healer of ills or worker
in wood, or even an inspired bard who can charm with his
song?" [4] The frame of reference here is, of course, the private,
purely secular feast, not a religious festival. But the traveling
ritual player—even the organized company, such as the Arioi
of the Society Islands and the Hula of Hawaii—is known from
much more primitive societies. Traveling artists were important
in Greece throughout its history. Plato's *Ion* takes its name
from a rhapsodist, Ion of Ephesus in Asia Minor. When the
dialogue opens, Ion tells Socrates that he has just come from
Epidaurus, where he won first prize for his Homeric recitation
at the quadrennial games to Asclepius, and that he fully expects
to be equally successful in the coming Panathenaic festival in
Athens.

The combination of oral transmission and lack of political
centralization could in time have led to many *Iliad*s, diverging
further and further from the "original." The temptation to
tamper with the text must have been great, on political grounds
alone. As the unchallenged authority on early history, Homer
was often an embarrassment—to the Athenians, for example,
whose pathetically small role in the great "national" war against
Troy was increasingly incommensurate with their ascending
role in Greek political affairs. But in her sharp sixth-century
struggle with Megara for control of the island of Salamis,

which dominates the Athenian harbor, Athens was able to justify her claim on historical grounds. "Ajax," says the *Iliad*, "brought twelve ships from Salamis, and bringing, he stationed them alongside the hosts of the Athenians." [5] To this Megara had but one answer—for neither the accuracy of Homer's history nor its relevance in territorial disputes was subject to question—and that was to charge forgery. The "and bringing" clause, said the Megarians, was a deliberate Athenian interpolation, not part of the genuine text at all.

In the Salamis case the Alexandrian scholars in later centuries tended to agree with Megara. The forger, they thought, was Pisistratus, tyrant of Athens from 560 to 527 B.C., who, together with Solon, had taken Salamis from Megara. Far more important, it was Pisistratus who was widely reputed to have settled the problem of an authentic Homeric text once and for all by having it fixed by experts and committed to writing in a formal edition, so to speak. There was a competing tradition which assigned this role to Solon, author of the great Athenian constitutional reform of 594 B.C. In the words of Diogenes Laertius, who wrote his *Lives and Opinions of Eminent Philosophers* in the third century after Christ, but who is here quoting a fourth-century B.C. author of a *Megarian History,* it was Solon who "prescribed that the rhapsodists shall recite Homer in fixed order, so that where the first leaves off, the next shall begin from that place." [6]

That there was a relatively ancient sixth-century Athenian recension at the root of our present texts of the *Iliad* and *Odyssey* seems to have been demonstrated from a close study of the dialect of the poems. There is some reason to accept the tradition that Pisistratus was the sponsor of that "edition." The attribution to Solon sounds suspiciously like a late effort

to transfer the credit from a tyrant to the man who had become
to the Greeks the counter-symbol, the constitutional, moderate
aristocrat, at once against tyranny and despotism and against
"mob rule."

A Pisistratean Homer poses two problems. The first and
simpler of the two is this: Our present texts of the poems derive
from medieval manuscripts, none earlier than the tenth century,
and from numerous fragments on papyrus, a few as old as the
third century B.C. How much was the text changed from the
time of Pisistratus, through copyists' errors, censorship, or any
of the other ills that plague all ancient texts in their transmission
by hand? The answer, based primarily on a comparison with
the extensive quotations from Homer in Plato, Aristotle, and
other Greek writers, is: substantially little; and remarkably
little indeed, apart from verbal changes of interest only to the
philologist.

But how close was the sixth-century Athenian edition to the
original? Here we have little to go on. One thing seems sure:
there was no excessive tampering with substance. The Athenian
editors may have permitted their own linguistic habits to creep
in now and then. Perhaps they even added the line about Ajax
lining up his twelve ships alongside the Athenians. But they
did not consciously modernize the poems, of that we can be
fairly certain, and they did not tailor the political implications
in any radical way to the needs of sixth-century Athenian
foreign affairs. Had they attempted to do so, they could scarcely
have succeeded. The poems were already too well known and
too deeply enshrined in the minds of the Greeks, and in a sense
in their religious emotions. Besides, sixth-century Athens
absolutely lacked the authority, political or intellectual, to

force a corrupted and distorted Homer on the other Hellenes. None of this is decisive, to be sure, but it permits the historian to work with his *Iliad* and his *Odyssey,* cautiously and always with suspicion, yet with a reasonable assurance that basically he is working with a fair approximation of eighth- and seventh-century poems.

Through all this dark history of the early transmission, public performance, and textual preservation of the poems, a key role may have been played by a group on the island of Chios who called themselves the Homerids, which means, literally, the descendants of Homer. They were professional rhapsodists, organized in a kind of guild and claiming direct descent from Homer. Their beginnings are lost, but they survived at least into the fourth century B.C., for Plato writes in his *Phaedrus:* "But some of the Homerids, I believe, recite two verses on Eros from the unpublished poems." [7] For all we know, the Homerids may in fact have been linked to "Homer" by kinship. Among modern Slavonic bards there are outstanding instances of transmittal of the skill within a family for several generations, and family specialization in various crafts is a common enough phenomenon in primitive and archaic societies. But it really matters little. Whether kin in fact or by accepted fiction, the Homerids were the recognized authorities on Homer for two or three centuries. And we may be sure that they would have been zealous in opposition to any effort, by Pisistratus or by anyone else, to undermine their superior knowledge and weaken their special professional position by producing a thoroughly rewritten text.

In one respect the Homerids themselves were able to introduce a false note. Commonly rhapsodists prefaced their recitations by short prologues, sometimes of their own composition. To that extent they represented a transitional form between the bard and the actor. As the recognized possessors of Homer's "unpublished writings," members of the Homerid guild could claim direct Homeric authorship for the prologues they wrote. The few which are still extant were collected in later antiquity and combined with five longer myth poems under a single title, *Homeric Hymns,* misleading in both its terms. Some of these thirty-three poems very probably originated among the Homerids in the seventh and sixth centuries B.C. The most extensive of them was addressed to Apollo; its first section closes with these highly personal lines:

"Remember me in after time whenever any one of men on earth, a stranger who has seen and suffered much, comes here and asks of you: 'Who think ye, girls, is the sweetest singer that comes here, and in whom do you most delight?' Then answer, each and all, with one voice: 'He is a blind man, and dwells in rocky Chios: his lays are evermore supreme.' As for me, I will carry your renown as far as I roam over the earth to the well-placed cities of man, and they will believe also; for indeed this thing is true." [8]

Even Thucydides, the most careful and in the best sense the most skeptical historian the ancient world ever produced, explicitly accepted Homer's authorship of this hymn, and the personal allusion of the final lines.[9] That was a truly astonishing error in judgment. The language of the "hymns" is Homeric, and the comparison ends right there; they are on a lower plane not only as literature but in their conceptual world, in their view of the gods.

"For indeed this thing is true." If the Greeks were pressed

to explain how their Homer, the blind minstrel, could sing truly of events four hundred years before his time, as they believed almost without an exception, they would have pointed to tradition handed down from generation to generation, and they would have pointed to the divine spark. "An inspired bard," said Eumaeus the swineherd; and the Greek word *thespis* means literally "produced or shown by a god." And *thespis* provides the necessary frame of reference for the opening line of the *Iliad:* "Sing, goddess, of the wrath of Peleus' son Achilles."

Hesiod began his *Theogony* with a longer introduction, in which the simple invocation has become a full-blown vision and personal revelation:

"And one day they (the Muses) taught Hesiod glorious song while he was shepherding his lambs under holy Helicon, and this word first the goddesses said to me . . . :

" 'Shepherds of the wilderness, wretched things of shame, mere bellies, we know how to speak many false things as though they were true; but we know, when we will, to utter true things.'

"So said the ready-voiced daughters of great Zeus, and they plucked and gave me a rod, a shoot of sturdy olive, a marvelous thing, and breathed into me a divine voice to celebrate things that shall be and things that were aforetime; and they bade me sing of the race of the blessed gods that are eternally, but ever to sing of themselves both first and last."

Hesiod's divine voice sounds like a direct quotation of the description of the soothsayer Calchas, "who knew things that were and things that shall be and things that were aforetime." [10] This close link between poetry and divine knowledge of the past and future found its personification in Orpheus, the sweet singer of legend in whose name a mass of mystical and magical writing piled up through the centuries. As if to underscore the point, when the Greeks came to give Homer a genealogy, as inevitably they would, they traced his ancestry back ten generations, precisely to Orpheus.

It would be wrong to turn such things aside as mere poetic fancy. When the bard Phemius said in the *Odyssey*, "I am self-taught; the god has implanted in my heart songs of all kinds," [11] to the poet and his audience that meant what it said and was to be taken like everything else in the poem, like the story of Odysseus and the Cyclops, or of Odysseus identifying himself by his ability to wield the bow no one else had the strength to pull. The best witness is Odysseus himself. In the palace of King Alcinous of the Phaeacians, where the hero had appeared incognito, there was a bard named Demodocus, to whom "God had given the art of song above all others." [12] After he had told various tales about the Trojan War, Odysseus said to him: "Demodocus, I praise you above all mortal men, whether it was the Muse, daughter of Zeus, who instructed you, or indeed Apollo. For you sing truly indeed of the fate of the Achaeans . . . as if you yourself had been present or had heard it from another." [13] Earlier Demodocus's precise knowledge had already been explained: "For so Phoebus Apollo had told him in prophecy." [14]

Still another echo is available, in a man who neither knew of Homer nor shared his inherited formulas, a nineteenth-century Kara-Kirghiz bard from the region north of the Hindu Kush: "I can sing every song; for God has planted the gift of song in my heart. He gives me the word on my tongue without my having to seek it. I have not learned any of my songs; everything springs up from my inner being, from myself." [15]

The historian's verdict, obviously, can rest neither on faith in the divine origin of the poems nor on the once common notion that sufficient antiquity is a proper warrant of truth—"we have the certainty that old and wise men held them to be true," says the preface to the *Heimskringla,* the saga of the Norse kings.[16] The historian, having established the point that neither the *Iliad* nor the *Odyssey* was essentially contemporary in outlook, must then examine their validity as pictures of the past. Was there ever a time in Greece when men lived as the poems tell (after they are stripped of supernatural intervention and superhuman capacities)? But first, was there a Trojan War?

Everyone knows the exciting story of Heinrich Schliemann, the German merchant with a vision and a love for the language of Homer, who dug in the soil of Asia Minor and rediscovered the city of Troy. Some three miles from the Dardanelles, at a place now called Hissarlik, there was one of the mounds that are the almost certain signs of ancient habitation. By careful analysis of topographical detail in ancient writings, Schliemann concluded that under this mound were the remains of the city of Ilion, which later Greeks had established on what they thought was the site of Troy and which outlived the Roman Empire for a good many centuries. When he tunneled into the mound he found layers of ruins, the oldest of which, we now know, dates from about 3000 B.C., and two bore unmistakable signs of violent destruction. One of these layers, the seventh according to more recent excavators, was no doubt the city of Priam and Hector. The historicity of the Homeric tale had been demonstrated archaeologically.

It is a shame to upset such a pretty and rare success story, but there are enough disturbing facts to compel the conclusion that "there is something wrong either with Schliemann's Troy

or with Homer's." [17] Without entering into technical archaeological analysis, we may point to the battle terrain. The *Iliad*
is filled with details, for that is the stuff of heroic narrative.
Basically they are so consistent that a serviceable map of the
area can be drawn from the poet's specifications. That map
and the region of Hissarlik fail to coincide, and the discrepancies are so crucial that it has been proved impossible to
recreate essential scenes of the *Iliad* on the actual site.

More interesting than the disappearance of the city is the
total disappearance of the Trojans themselves. To begin with,
as a nationality in the *Iliad* they are quite without distinguish-
ing characteristics. They are as Greek and as heroic as their
opponents in every respect. If the opening line of the *Iliad*
introduces Achilles, the closing line bids farewell to Hector, the
chief Trojan hero: "Thus they performed the funeral rites for
Hector, tamer of horses." Hector is a Greek name (unlike the
name of Hector's father, Priam), and as late as the middle of the
second century after Christ travelers who came to Thebes in
Boeotia on the Greek mainland were shown his tomb, near the
Fountain of Oedipus, and were told how his bones had been
brought from Troy at the behest of the Delphic oracle. This
typical bit of fiction must mean that there was an old Theban
hero Hector, a Greek, whose myths antedated the Homeric
poems. Even after Homer had located Hector in Troy for all
time, the Thebans held on to their hero, and the Delphic oracle
provided the necessary sanction.

Among the Trojan allies there were peoples who were certainly non-Greek. It was for one of them, the Carians, that the
poet reserved the epithet *barbarophonoi* (barbarous-talking,
that is, unintelligible). The Carians are well known historically;

the tomb of their fourth-century king, Mausolus, gives us our word *mausoleum*. Other Trojan allies are also historically identifiable, and that serves to underscore the curious fact that the Trojans themselves, like Achilles' Myrmidons, have vanished so completely. Even if we were to accept the ancient explanation for the disappearance of the city, that it was so thoroughly demolished by the victors that "there is no certain trace of walls" [18]—which would involve us in new difficulties with Schliemann and his successors, who found traces of walls —it is hard to discover a parallel for the mysterious failure of the people themselves to leave any traces.

On the Greek side there is a high correlation between the important place names given in the *Iliad* and the centers of the so-called Mycenaean civilization rediscovered by modern archaeologists, although the poverty of the finds in Odysseus' Ithaca is a notable exception. This civilization flourished in Greece in the period 1400–1200 B.C., and here the name of Schliemann as the first discoverer must remain unchallenged. But again Homer and archaeology part company quickly. On the whole, he knew where the Mycenaean civilization flourished, and his heroes lived in great Bronze Age palaces unknown in Homer's own day. And that is virtually all he knew about Mycenaean times, for the catalogue of his errors is very long. His arms bear a resemblance to the armor of his time, quite unlike the Mycenaean, although he persistently casts them in antiquated bronze, not iron. His gods had temples, and the Mycenaeans built none, whereas the latter constructed great vaulted tombs in which to bury their chieftains, and the poet cremates his. A neat little touch is provided by the battle chariots. Homer had heard of them, but he did not really vis-

ualize what one did with chariots in a war. So his heroes
normally drove from their tents a mile or less away, carefully
dismounted, and then proceeded to battle on foot.

The key to the Homeric confusion lies in the bardic technique.
The raw materials of the poem were the mass of inherited formulas, and as they passed through generations of bards they
underwent change after change, partly by deliberate act of the
poets, whether for artistic reasons or from more prosaic political
considerations, and partly by carelessness and indifference to
historical accuracy, compounded by the errors that are inevitable in oral transmission. That there was a Mycenaean
kernel in the *Iliad* and *Odyssey* cannot be doubted, but it was
small and what little there was of it was distorted beyond sense
or recognition. Often the material was self-contradictory, yet
that was no bar to its use. Poetic convention demanded traditional formulas, and neither the bard nor his audience checked
the details. The man who started it all by abducting Helen is
named both Alexander, which is Greek, and Paris, which is
not (just as his city had two names, Ilion and Troy); he is both
a contemptible, unheroic coward and a true hero. As usual,
later generations began to seek explanations, but not the poet
of the *Iliad*.

We may take it for granted that there was a Trojan War in
Mycenaean times; more correctly, that there were many Trojan
wars. War was normal in that world, and the Achchiyava reference in Hittite records shows that the ancestors of the Hellenes
of history fought in Asia Minor. It is even conceivable that the
war was fought over a woman. "The people of Asia," says
Herodotus, "when their women were seized, made no issue of
it, whereas the Greeks, on account of a single Lacedaemonian

woman, collected a great expedition, came to Asia, and destroyed the power of Priam." [19]

But a ten-year war, or a war of any smaller number of years, is out of the question. "Would that I were in the prime of youth and my might as steadfast as when a quarrel broke out between us and the Eleans over a cattle raid. . . . Exceedingly abundant was then the booty we drove out of the plain together, fifty herds of cattle, as many flocks of sheep, as many droves of swine, as many wide herds of goats, and a hundred and fifty bays, all mares. . . . And Neleus was glad at heart that so much booty fell to me the first time I went to war." [20]

This was a typical "war" as narrated by Nestor, a raid for booty. Even if repeated year after year, these wars remained single raids. There is a scene in the third book of the *Iliad* in which Helen sits alongside Priam on the battlements of Troy and identifies Agamemnon, Odysseus, and a few other Achaean heroes for the old king. That could make sense at the beginning of the war; it can make no sense in the tenth year (unless we are prepared to believe that the poet could find no better device by which to introduce some details of no great importance). It could also make sense in a brief war, and perhaps this is an illustration of the way in which one traditional piece of the story was retained after the war had ballooned into ten years and the piece had become rationally incongruous. While the war was growing, furthermore, the bards neglected to make proper arrangements for recruits to replace the fallen men, for the feeding of besiegers and besieged, or for the establishment of some sort of communication between the battlefield and the home bases of the Greeks.

The glorification of insignificant incidents is common in

heroic poetry. The French *Song of Roland* tells of a great battle at Roncevaux in the year 778 A.D., between the hosts of Charlemagne and the Saracens. Like Homer, the poet of the French epic is unknown, but he certainly lived in the twelfth century, at the time of the Crusades. Unlike Homer, he could read and he had access to chronicles, which he explicitly says he used. But the facts are these: the actual battle of Roncevaux was a minor engagement in the Pyrenees between a small detachment of Charlemagne's army and some Basque raiders. It was neither important nor crusade-like. The twelve Saracen chieftains of the poem and their army of 400,000 are pure invention; some even have German or Byzantine names. And all the details of the background are wrong.

The *Song of Roland* can be checked against written records. The *Iliad* and the *Odyssey* cannot, and, insofar as historical detail is concerned, there is no way of reversing the process of distortion and re-establishing the original kernel. Comparison with other examples of the genre leads to what Rhys Carpenter has called the "theorem . . . that the more an oral poet seems to know about a distant event the less he really knows about it and the more certainly he is inventing." [21]

The *Song of Roland* also shares another negative with the *Iliad* and *Odyssey*. It is not contemporary in its social conditions, its politics, and its details of wars and warriors. Not that it lacks realism. On the contrary, it is of the essence of heroic poetry that, "since heroes move in what is assumed to be a real world, their background and their circumstances must be depicted," always "with realism and objectivity." [22] Specifically, the background of Roland is the France of about a century before the poet's own time, as if the formulas and the traditions coming down from the days of Charlemagne froze about the year 1000 and then went on with little further change. This suggests what hints in Greek literature and comparative studies tend to confirm, that the Homeric picture is analogous. The world of Odysseus was not that of the seventh century B.C., neither was it the Mycenaean age five or six or seven hundred years earlier.* If it is to be placed in time, as everything we know about heroic poetry says it must, the most likely centuries seem to be the tenth and ninth. By then the long years of wandering and infiltration were over, the mixture of race and culture had been completed, the catastrophe that brought down Mycenaean civilization and made itself felt all over the eastern Mediterranean had been forgotten. The history of the Greeks as such had begun.

Essentially the picture of the background offered by the poems is a coherent one. Anachronistic fragments cling to it in spots, some too ancient and some, particularly in the *Odyssey,* too recent, a reflection of the poet's own time. For historical study, the accuracy of the background is quite separable from the demonstrable inaccuracy of the episodes and the narrative detail, the action. "Homer," wrote Aristotle, "is praiseworthy in many respects, and especially because he alone of poets perceives the part he should take himself. The poet should speak as little as possible in his own person. . . ." [23] But this technical virtue, become a vice to poets of another world, should not mislead us, as it did no less gifted a critic than Coleridge. "There is no subjectivity whatever in the Homeric

---

* Important new evidence for this conclusion comes from the widely publicized suggestion by Michael Ventris and John Chadwick that the language of the Mycenaean tablets is Greek. Their first tentative readings, published in the *Journal of Hellenic Studies* for 1953, reveal (if they are right) a world altogether unlike the Homeric, one that was materially far more advanced, as we already knew from the archaeology; and institutionally more complex and reminiscent of the ancient Near East.

poetry," was the judgment of Coleridge the romantic, neither
the "subjectivity of the poet, as of Milton, who is himself before
himself in everything he wrote," nor the "subjectivity of the
persona, or dramatic character, as in all Shakespeare's great
creations." [24] This standing at a distance from his characters
and their behavior, which is the mark of Homeric technique,
had nothing to do with indifference, with disinterest, with an
unwillingness to become involved. The poet transmitted his
inherited background materials with a deceptively cool precision. That enables us to treat his materials as the raw materials
for the study of a real world of real men, a world of history
and not of fiction. But it also besets our analysis with traps,
for the temptation is ever present to ignore the implications in
the poet's conscious selectivity and to brush aside apparent
confusions and contradictions in social or political matters (as
distinct from narrative incidents) as nothing more than the
carelessness of a bard who really did not care.

Of course there must be something of a historian's license
in pinning down the world of Odysseus to the tenth and ninth
centuries before Christ. And that license must extend still
further. There are sections in the poems, such as the tale of the
adultery of Ares and Aphrodite or the scene in Hades in the
final book of the *Odyssey,* which appear to have a later origin
than other sections. By license, we here ignore the distinction
for the most part, just as we sometimes speak of one Homer,
as if the *Iliad* and *Odyssey* were contemporaneous works, the
products of one man's creation. Some distortion results, but the
margin of error can be held to a rather acceptable minimum,
because the patterns we draw rest on an over-all analysis of
the poems, not on any one single verse, segment, or narrative
incident; because all parts, early or late, were built so much

from the old formulas; and because later Greek history and the study of other societies together offer a great measure of control. It is convenience, finally, rather than license, that suggests retention of the ten-year war, and of Achilles and Hector and Odysseus and all the other famous names, as useful labels for unknown King X and Chieftain Y.

~~~~~~

CHAPTER III

Wealth and Labor

In the second book of the *Iliad* the poet catalogues the contending hosts, in the case of the Greeks by the names of their chief leaders and the number of ships each brought with him. "But the multitude (i.e., the commoners) I could not relate nor name, not if I had ten tongues, nor ten mouths." [1] The list totals 1186 ships, which, at a minimum computation, means over 60,000 men, a figure as trustworthy as the 400,000 Saracens of *The Song of Roland*. The world of Odysseus was a small one in numbers of people. There are no statistics and no ways of making good guesses, but the five-acre sites of the archaeologists, together with what is known from later centuries, leave no doubt that the populations of the individual communities were to be reckoned in four figures, often even in three, and that the numbers in the poems, whether of ships or flocks or slaves or nobles, are unrealistic and invariably err on the side of exaggeration.

One of the smallest contingents in the catalogue of ships was led by Odysseus, a mere twelve (Agamemnon had one hundred and provided sixty others for the inland Arcadians). He is announced as king of the Cephallenians, who inhabit three adjacent islands in the Ionian Sea, Cephallenia, Ithaca, and Zacynthus, together with two sites apparently on the nearby mainland. But it is with Ithaca specifically that he is always directly identified. And it is on the island of Ithaca, not in the Never-Never Land through which he later wandered, that the world of Odysseus can chiefly be examined.

The island population was dominated by a group of noble families, some of whose men participated in the expedition against Troy, while others remained at home. Among the latter was Mentor, to whose watchful eye Odysseus entrusted his young wife, Penelope, who came from another land, and his only child, his newborn son Telemachus, when he himself went off. For twenty years there was a strange hiatus in the political leadership of Ithaca. Odysseus' father, Laertes, did not resume the throne, though still alive. Penelope could not rule, being a woman. Mentor was no guardian in any legal sense, merely a well-intentioned, ineffectual figure, and he did not function as a regent.

For ten years a similar situation prevailed throughout the Greek world, while the kings, with few exceptions, were at war. With the destruction of Troy and the great homecoming of the heroes, life was resumed in its normal ways. The fallen kings were replaced; some who returned, like Agamemnon, ran into usurpers and assassins; and the others came back to the seats of power and its pursuits. But for Odysseus there was a different fate. Having offended the god Poseidon, he was tossed about for another ten years before he was rescued, largely through the intervention of Athena, and permitted to return to Ithaca. It was this second decade that perplexed the people at home. No one in all Hellas knew what had befallen Odysseus, whether he had died on the return journey from Troy or was still alive

somewhere in the outer world. This uncertainty laid the basis
for the second theme of the poem, the story of the suitors.

Again there is trouble with numbers. No less than 108 nobles,
56 from Ithaca and the other islands ruled by Odysseus, and
52 from a neighboring mainland kingdom, says the poet, were
paying court to Penelope. She was to be forced to choose
Odysseus' successor from among them. This was no ordinary
wooing, ancient style or modern. Except that they continued to
sleep in their own homes, the suitors had literally taken over
the household of the absent Odysseus and were steadily eating
and drinking their way through his vast stores; "not twenty
men together have so much wealth," according to the swineherd Eumaeus.[2] For three years Penelope defended herself by
delaying tactics, but her power of resistance was wearing down.
The ceaseless carouse in the house, the growing certainty that
Odysseus would never return, and the suitors' open threat,
made publicly to Telemachus, "to eat up your livelihood and
your possessions," [3] were having their effect. Just in time Odysseus returned, disguised as a wandering beggar. By employing
all his craft and prowess, and a little magic, he succeeded in
slaughtering the suitors, and, with the final intervention of
Athena, in re-establishing his position as head of his household and king in Ithaca.

Abroad, Odysseus' life was one long series of struggles with
witches, giants, and nymphs, but there is none of that in the
Ithacan story. On the island we are confronted with human
society alone (including the ever-present Athena, to be sure,
but in a sense the Greek gods were always a part of human
society, working through dreams, prophecies, oracles, and
other signs). The same is true of the *Iliad*. For the story of the
few days between the insult by Agamemnon and the death of

Hector at the hands of Achilles, as for the main plot of the Ithacan theme, the nobility provides all the characters. The *Odyssey* parades other people of the island, but largely as stage props or stock types: Eumaeus the swineherd, the old nurse Eurycleia, Phemius the bard, the nameless "carvers of the meat," the sailors and housemaids and miscellaneous retainers. The poet's meaning is clear: on the field of battle, as in the power struggle which is the Ithacan theme, only the aristocrats had roles.

A deep horizontal cleavage marked the world of the Homeric poems. Above the line were the *aristoi*, literally the "best people," the hereditary nobles who held most of the wealth and all the power, in peace as in war. Below were all the others, for whom there was no collective technical term, the multitude. The gap between the two was rarely crossed, except by the inevitable accidents of wars and raids. The economy was such that the creation of new fortunes, and thereby of new nobles, was out of the question. Marriage was strictly class-bound, so that the other door to social advancement was also securely locked.

Below the main line there were various other divisions, but, unlike the primary distinction between aristocrat and commoner, they seem blurred and they are often indefinable. Not even so simple a contrast as that between slave and free man stands out in sharp clarity. The word *drester*, for example, which means "one who works or serves," is used in the *Odyssey* for the free and the unfree alike. The work they did and the treatment they received, at the hands of their masters as in the psychology of the poet, are often indistinguishable.

Slaves existed in number; they were property, disposable at will. More precisely, there were slave women, for wars and raids were the main source of supply, and there was little ground, economic or moral, for sparing the lives of the defeated men. The heroes as a rule killed the males and carried off the females, regardless of rank. Before offering up his prayer for his son, Hector, who knew his own doom, said to his wife: "But I care not so much for the grief of the Trojans here-after . . . as for yours, when one of the bronze-clad Achaeans will carry you off in tears; and you will be in Argos, working the loom at another woman's bidding, and you will draw water from Messeis or Hypereia, most unwillingly, and great con-straint will be laid upon you." [4]

Hector did not need Apollo's aid in foretelling the future. Never in Greek history was it otherwise; the persons and the property of the vanquished belonged to the victor, to be dis-posed of as he chose. But Hector showed gentle restraint, for his prophecy was not complete. The place of slave women was in the household, washing, sewing, cleaning, grinding meal, valeting. If they were young, however, their place was also in the master's bed. Of the old nurse Eurycleia, the poet reports that "Laertes bought her with (some of) his possessions when she was still in the prime of youth . . . but he never had in-tercourse with her in bed, and he avoided the anger of his wife." [5] It was the rarity of Laertes' behavior, and the promise of his wife's wrath, that warranted the special comment. Neither custom nor morality demanded such abstinence.

It is idle to seek for numbers here. Odysseus is reported to have had fifty female slaves, but that is surely a convenient round figure, used for the household of King Alcinous of the Phaeacians too. A few men were also in bondage, such as the swineherd Eumaeus, an aristocrat by birth, who had been kidnaped when a child by Phoenician traders and sold into slavery. Like the women, the male slaves worked in the home, and in the fields and vineyards, never abroad as servants or orderlies.

Of the Ithacans who were not slaves, the free population who were the bulk of the community, some were surely independent householders, free herders and peasants with their own holdings (although the poet tells us nothing about them). Others were specialists, carpenters and metal workers, soothsayers, bards, and physicians. Because they supplied certain essential needs in a way that neither the lords nor the nonspecialists among their followers could match, these men, a handful in numbers, floated in mid-air in the social hierarchy. Seers and physicians might even be nobles, but the others, though they were close to the aristocratic class and even shared its life in many respects, were decidedly not of the aristocracy, as the treatment and behavior of the bard Phemius attest.

Eumaeus, we remember, called these specialists *demioergoi,* literally "those who work for the people" (and once Penelope attached the same classificatory label to the heralds). From the word, used in the Homeric poems only in these two passages, it has been suggested that the *demioergoi* operated in a way well known among primitive and archaic groups, the Kabyle of Algiers, for instance: "Another specialist is the blacksmith, who is also an outsider. The villagers lend him a house, and each family pays him a fixed portion of his yearly salary in grain and other produce." [6] Unfortunately the evidence for the world of Odysseus is far from clear or decisive. Once when Nestor, at home, wished to make sacrifice, he ordered his servants, " 'Bid the goldsmith Laerces come here, that he may gild the horns of the cow'. . . . And the smith came, with the smith's tools in his hands, the instruments of his craft, anvil

and hammer and well-made fire-tongs, with which he worked
the gold. . . . And the old horseman Nestor gave gold, and
the smith then skillfully gilded the horns." [7] Neither the status
of the goldsmith nor even his domicile is indicated here, unlike the passage in the *Iliad* about the great "unwrought mass
of iron" which Achilles offered from his booty for a weight-
throwing contest. The iron was to be both the test and the
prize for the winner. He will have it, said Achilles, "to use
for five full years, for neither the shepherd nor the plowman
will have to go into town for lack of iron, but this will furnish
it." [8]

Although nothing is ever said about remuneration, it does
not necessarily follow that each family in the community gave
the smith, or the other *demioergoi,* a fixed annual maintenance
quota. They could have been paid as they worked, provided
only that they were available to the public, to the whole *demos*.
That availability would explain the word well enough.

Eumaeus indicated still another special quality of the *demioergoi* when he asked "who ever summons a stranger from
abroad . . . unless he be one of the *demioergoi*" (again with
a parallel among the Kabyle). Were they, then, traveling tink-
ers and minstrels, going from community to community on a
more or less fixed schedule? Actually the logic of Eumaeus's
question is that all invited strangers are craftsmen, not that
all craftsmen are strangers. Probably some were and some were
not, and, of those who were, none need have worked on a cir-
cuit at all. The heralds were certainly permanent, regular, full-
scale members of the community. The bards may have wandered a bit (in the poet's own day they traveled all the time).
Regarding the others, we are simply not informed.

Indispensable as the *demioergoi* were, their contribution to the quantity of work performed on an estate was a very small one. For the basic work of pasturage and tillage in the fields, of stewardship and service in the house, there was no need of specialists: every man in Ithaca could herd and plow and carve, and those commoners who had their own holdings worked them themselves. Others made up the permanent staffs of Odysseus and the nobles, free men like the unnamed "carvers of the meat," who were an integral part of the household. Still others, the least fortunate, were *thetes,* unattached, property-less laborers who worked for hire and begged what they could not steal.

"Stranger," said the leading suitor Eurymachus to the beggar (Odysseus in disguise), "would you be willing to work as a *thes,* if I should take you in my service, on a farm at the border—you can be sure of pay—laying walls and planting tall trees? There I would furnish you ample grain and put clothes on your back and give you shoes for your feet." Ample grain and clothes and shoes made up the store of a commoner's goods. But Eurymachus was mocking, "creating laughter among his companions," at the direct inspiration of Athena, who "would by no means permit the arrogant suitors to refrain from heart-rending scorn, so that the pain might sink still more deeply into the heart of Odysseus son of Laertes." [9]

A little of the joke lay in the words, "you can be sure of pay." No *thes* could be sure. Poseidon once angrily demanded of Apollo why he of all the gods should be so completely on the side of the Trojans. Have you forgotten, Poseidon asked, how, on order from Zeus, "we worked as *thetes* for one year, for an agreed-upon pay," for Laomedon, king of Troy, building the wall around the city and herding cattle? And how, at the end of the year, Laomedon "deprived us of our pay and sent us off with threats?" [10] The real joke, however, the utter scornfulness of Eurymachus's proposal, lay in the offer itself, not in the hint that the pay would be withheld in the end. To see the whole point, we turn to Achilles in Hades rather than to Poseidon on Olympus. "Do not speak to me lightly of death, glorious Odysseus," said the shade of Achilles. "I would rather be bound down, working as a *thes* for another, by the side of a landless man, whose livelihood was not great, than be ruler over all the dead who have perished." [11]

A *thes*, not a slave, was the lowest creature on earth that Achilles could think of. The terrible thing about a *thes* was his lack of attachment, his not belonging. The authoritarian household, the *oikos*, was the center around which life was organized, from which flowed not only the satisfaction of material needs, including security, but ethical norms and values, duties, obligations, and responsibilities, social relationships, and relations with the gods. The *oikos* was not merely the family, it was all the people of the household and its goods; hence "economics" (from the Latinized form, *oecus*), the art of managing an *oikos*, meant running a farm, not managing to keep peace in the family.

Just what it meant, in terms of customary or legal obligation and in a man's own familial life, to be a permanent but free member of the *oikos* of another is by no means clear. Negatively it meant considerable loss of freedom of choice and of mobility. Yet these men were neither slaves nor serfs nor bondsmen. They were retainers (*therapontes*), exchanging their service for a proper place in the basic social unit, the household—a vicarious membership, no doubt, but one that gave them both material security and the psychological values and satisfactions that went with belonging. Altogether the chief aristocrats managed, by a combination of slaves, chiefly female, and a whole hierarchy of retainers, supplemented by *thetes,* to build up very imposing and very useful household forces, equipped to do whatever was required of a man of status and power in their world. The hierarchy of retainers, it should be added, reached very high indeed. As a child Patroclus was forced to flee his home. Peleus received him in his palace and "named him retainer" of young Achilles.[12] The analogy that comes to mind at once is that of the noble page in some early modern court, just as "lord Eteoneus, the ready retainer of Menelaus" who met guests at the door and poured the wine for them, might well have been the counterpart of a Lord Chamberlain.[13]

A *thes* in Ithaca might even have been an Ithacan, not an outsider. But he was no part of an *oikos,* and in this respect even the slave was better off. The slave, human but nevertheless a part of the property element of the *oikos,* was altogether a nice symbol of the situation. Only twice does Homer use the word that later became standard in Greek for a slave, *doulos,* which seems etymologically tied to the idea of labor. Otherwise his word is *dmos,* with its obvious link with *doma* or *domos,* a house; and after Homer and Hesiod *dmos* never appears in literature apart from a few instances of deliberate archaizing, as in Sophocles and Euripides. The treatment of the slaves was essentially milder and more humane than the pattern familiar from plantation slavery. Eumaeus, a favorite slave, had even been able to purchase a slave for himself. To be sure, a dozen of the slave girls were hanged in the midst of the carnage of Odysseus' successful return, but it was the method of their execution alone that distinguished them from the lordly suitors, who died by the bow and the spear.

There was little mating of slave with slave because there were so few males among them. Nearly all the children born to the slave women were the progeny of the master or of other free males in the household. Commonly, in many different social systems, as among the Greeks later on, such offspring were slaves like their mothers: "the belly holds the child," say the Tuareg nomads of the Sahara in explanation. Not so in the world of Odysseus, where it was the father's status that was determinative. Thus, in the fanciful tale with which Odysseus sought to conceal his identity from Eumaeus immediately upon his return to Ithaca, his father was a wealthy Cretan, his mother a "bought concubine." When the father died the legitimate sons divided the property, giving him only a dwelling and a few goods. Later, by his valor, he obtained to wife the daughter of "a man of many estates." [14] The slave woman's son might sometimes be a second-class member of the family, but even then he was part of that narrower circle within the *oikos* as a whole, free and without even the stigma of bastardy in our sense, let alone the mark of slavery.

Fundamentally the difference between the ordinary landowner and the noble lay in the magnitude of their respective *oikoi,* and therefore in the numbers of retainers they could support, which, translated into practical terms, meant in their power. Superficially the difference was one of birth. At some past point, remote or near in time, either conquest or wealth created the original separation. Then it froze, continued along hereditary lines, was given divine sanction through genealogies that assigned every noble family a god for an ancestor, and was called a blood-distinction.

The nature of the economy served to seal and preserve the class line. Wherever the wealth of the household is so decisive,

unless there is a measure of mobility in wealth, unless the opportunity exists to create new fortunes, the structure becomes
caste-like in its rigidity. This was the case in Ithaca. The base
of the *oikos* was its land, and there was no way, under normal,
peaceful conditions, to acquire new land in the settled regions.
Hypothetically one might push to the frontier and take up
vacant land, but few men actually did anything so absurd and
foolhardy, except under the most violent compulsions. It was
not out of mere sentiment for the fatherland that banishment
was deemed the bitterest of fates. The exile was stripped of all
ties that meant life itself; it made no difference in this regard
whether one had been compelled to flee or had gone from
home in the search for land by free choice.

The primary use of the land was in pasturage. To begin the
story of his adventure among the Cyclopes, which he told at
the court of Alcinous, Odysseus underscored the primitive
savagery of the one-eyed giants. First of all, they had not
learned the art of agriculture: "they neither plant anything nor
till." [15] Nevertheless, Odysseus' own world was one of pasturage, not of tillage (unlike the Greek world at the time of Homer
himself and of Hesiod, when agriculture had moved to the
fore). Greek soil is poor, rocky and waterless, so that no more
than twenty per cent of the total surface of the peninsula can
be cultivated. In places it once provided excellent pasturage
for horses and cattle; virtually all of it is still, in our day, good
for the smaller animals, sheep and pigs and goats. The households of the poems carried on a necessary minimum of plowing and planting, especially on orchard and vine-land, but it
was their animals on which they depended for clothing, draft,
transport, and much of their food.

With their flocks and their labor force, with plentiful stone for building and clay for pots, the great households could almost realize their ideal of absolute self-sufficiency. The *oikos* was above all a unit of consumption. Its activities, insofar as they were concerned with the satisfaction of material wants, were guided by one principle, to meet the consuming needs of the lord and his people; if possible by the products of his estates, supplemented by booty. But there was one thing which prevented full self-sufficiency, a need which could neither be eliminated nor satisfied by substitutes, and that was the need for metal. Scattered deposits existed in Greece, but the main sources of supply were outside, in western Asia and central Europe.

Metal meant tools and weapons, but it also meant something else, perhaps as important. When Telemachus had concluded his visit at the palace of Menelaus in Sparta, in search of news about his father, his host offered him, as a parting gift, "three horses and a chariot-board of polished metal and . . . a fine goblet." The young man demurred. "And whatever gift you would give me, let it be treasure. I will not take horses to Ithaca. . . . In Ithaca there are neither wide courses nor any meadowland." [16] The Greek word customarily rendered by "treasure" is *keimelion*, literally something that can be laid away. In the poems treasure was of bronze, iron, or gold, less often of silver or fine cloth, and usually it was shaped into goblets, tripods, or caldrons. Such objects had some utilitarian worth and they could provide aesthetic satisfaction too, but neither function was of real moment compared to their value as symbolic wealth or prestige wealth. The twin uses of treasure were in possessing it and in giving it away, paradoxical as that may appear. Until the appropriate occasion for a gift presented itself, most treasure was kept hidden under lock and key. It was not "used" in the narrow sense of that word.

When Agamemnon was finally persuaded that appeasement of Achilles was absolutely essential to prevent the destruction of the Achaean forces, he went about it by offering amends through gifts. His offer included some to be presented at once, others on conditions of victory. And what a catalogue it was: seven cities, a daughter to wife with a great dowry "such as no one ever yet gave with his daughter," the girl Briseis, over whom the quarrel had broken out, seven captive women from Lesbos skilled in crafts, twelve prize-winning racehorses, and his choice of twenty Trojan women when the war was won. These, apart from the horses, were the utilitarian gifts. But Agamemnon began with none of them; first came "seven tripods that have never been on the fire and ten talents of gold and twenty glittering caldrons," and further on, from the anticipated Trojan spoils, as much gold and bronze as his ship would hold.* That was treasure, and its high importance is marked by the care with which it is enumerated here and again later in the poem. Menelaus's gift to Telemachus, all treasure, reappears four more times in the *Odyssey,* in three different books.

Whatever its purpose or its source, metal created for the individual *oikos* a special problem in the distribution of goods. For the most part distribution was internal and hence no problem at all. Since there has never been a world of Robinson

* *Iliad* 9.121–56. In Plato's will, preserved by Diogenes Laertius, *Lives* 3.41–43, the itemized bequest included "three minas of silver, a silver bowl weighing 165 drachmas, a small cup weighing 45 drachmas, a gold ring and gold earring weighing 4½ drachmas together." This is treasure, now narrowed to gold and silver, and, like Agamemnon's it is made up indifferently of metal and metal objects.

Crusoes, the simplest human groups perforce have a mechanism, and it is the same one that served, with some extension,
even the most elaborate princely *oikos*. All the productive
work, the seeding and harvesting and milling and weaving,
even the hunting and raiding, though performed by individuals,
was carried on in behalf of the household as a whole. The final
products, ready for consumption, were gathered and stored
centrally, and from the center they were redistributed—in the
authoritarian household, by its head at a time and in a measure
he deemed appropriate.

It made no difference in essence whether the family members within the household were no more than a husband, wife,
and child, or whether the *oikos* was that of King Priam of Troy,
with his fifty sons and their wives, twelve daughters and their
husbands, and his uncounted grandchildren; or the more reasonable example of Nestor at Pylos, with six sons and some
sons-in-law. The sons possessed arms and treasure of their own,
from gifts and booty, as the wives and daughters had their
fine garments and jewels. But unless the males left the paternal
household and established their own *oikoi*, their personal property was an essentially insignificant factor. Normally, the poems
seem to say, although the evidence is not altogether clear and
consistent, the sons remained with their father in his lifetime.

Architecturally the heart of the system was the storeroom.
Preparing for his journey to Pylos, Telemachus "went down to
his father's spacious, high-ceilinged storeroom, where gold and
copper lay piled up, and clothing in chests, and fragrant oil
in plenty; and there stood jars of wine, old and sweet, filled
with the unmixed divine drink, close together in a row along
the wall." [17] And of course it contained arms and grain in
quantity. More than three hundred years after Homer the

Athenian Xenophon, a gentleman farmer and no tribal chieftain or king, still placed proper care of the storeroom high on
the list of wifely virtues.

It was when distribution had to cross *oikos* lines that the
creation of new and special devices became necessary. Wars
and raids for booty, indistinguishable in the eyes of Odysseus'
world, were organized affairs, often involving a combination
of families, occasionally even of communities. Invariably there
was a captain, one of whose functions was to act as the head
and distribute the booty, all of which was first brought to a
central storage point. Division was by lot, much like the division
of an inheritance when there were several heirs. For example,
not all of Odysseus' homecoming adventures were tragic. Two
or three times he and his men had the pleasant opportunity to
raid. "From Ilion," he began the account of his wanderings,
"the wind bore me near to the Cicones, to Ismarus. There I
sacked the city and killed the men; taking the women and
many goods, we divided them, so that no one might go cheated
of his equal share through me." [18]

Forcible seizure, followed by distribution in this fashion,
was one way to acquire metal or other goods from an outside
source. Some scholars think that the kernel of historical truth
in the tale of the Trojan War is precisely such a mass raid for
iron supplies. Whether they are right or not, there were surely
many smaller Trojan wars to such a purpose, against Greeks
as well as against barbarians. But the violent solution was
neither always feasible nor even always desirable; if the aggrieved party were strong enough it invited retaliation, and
there were times and conditions when even the fiercest of the
heroes preferred peace. An exchange mechanism was then the
only alternative, and the basic one was gift-exchange. This was

no Greek invention. On the contrary, it is the basic organizing mechanism among many primitive peoples, as in the Trobriand Islands, where "most if not all economic acts are found to belong to some chain of reciprocal gifts and counter-gifts." [19]

The word "gift" is not to be misconstrued. It may be stated as a flat rule of both primitive and archaic society that no one ever gave anything, whether goods or services or honors, without proper recompense, real or wishful, immediate or years away, to himself or to his kin. The act of giving was, therefore, in an essential sense always the first half of a reciprocal action, the other half of which was a counter-gift.

Not even the parting gift was an exception, although in this one instance there was an element of risk. The last of the recognition scenes in the *Odyssey*, between the hero and his aged father, began in the customary fashion, with Odysseus claiming to be someone else, a stranger from another land in search of information about "Odysseus." Your son, he said to Laertes, visited me about five years ago and received the proper gifts. "Of well-wrought gold I gave him seven talents, and I gave him a bowl with flower designs, all of silver, and twelve single cloaks and as many carpets and as many fine mantles, and as many tunics besides, and in addition four pretty women skilled in excellent work." Laertes wept, for he had long been satisfied that his son had perished, and he could think of no better way to reveal that fact to the stranger than by commenting on the gift situation. "The countless gifts which you gave, you bestowed in vain. For if you had found that man still alive in the land of Ithaca, he would have sent you on your way well provided with gifts in return." [20]

Then there is the interesting scene in the opening book of the *Odyssey*, in which the goddess Athena appeared to Telemachus in the shape of Mentes, a Taphian chieftain. When she was ready to part, the young man followed the expected custom: "Go to your ship happy in your heart, bearing a gift, valuable and very beautiful, which will be your treasure from me, such as dear guest-friends give to guest-friends." * This created a very delicate situation for the goddess. One did not refuse a proffered gift, yet she could not accept it under the false pretense of her human disguise. (Gods as gods not only accepted gifts from mortals, they expected and demanded them.) Being the cleverest of the gods, Athena unhesitatingly found the perfect solution. "Do not detain me any longer as I am eager to be on my way. The gift, which the heart of a friend prompts you to give me, give it to me on my return journey that I may carry it home; choose a very beautiful one, that will bring you a worthy one in exchange." 21

Telemachus had said nothing about a counter-gift. Yet he and "Mentes" understood each other perfectly: the counter-gift was as expected as the original gift at parting. That was what gift-giving was in this society. The return need not be forthcoming at once, and it might take several forms. But come it normally would. "In a society ruled by respect for the past, a traditional gift is very near indeed to an obligation." 22 No single detail in the life of the heroes receives so much attention in the *Iliad* and the *Odyssey* as gift-giving, and always there is frank reference to adequacy, appropriateness, recompense. "But then Zeus son of Cronus took from Glaucus his wits, in that he exchanged golden armor with Diomedes son of Tydeus for one of bronze, the worth of a hundred oxen for the worth of nine oxen." 23 The poet's editorial comment, so rare for him, reflects the magnitude of Glaucus's mistake in judgment.

* "Guest-friend" is explained in the latter part of Chapter IV.

There was scarcely a limit to the situations in which gift-giving was operative. More precisely, the word "gift" was a cover-all for a great variety of actions and transactions which later became differentiated and acquired their own appellations. There were payments for services rendered, desired, or anticipated; what we would call fees, rewards, prizes, and sometimes bribes. The formulaic material was rich in such references, as in the lines with which Telemachus and twice Penelope responded to a stranger's favorable interpretation of a sign from the gods: "Stranger, would that these words be fulfilled! Speedily should you become aware of friendship and many gifts from me, so that whoever met you would congratulate you." [24]

Then there were taxes and other dues to lords and kings, amends with a penal overtone (Agamemnon's gift to Achilles), and even ordinary loans—and again the Homeric word is always "gift." Defending himself for having lent Telemachus a ship with which to sail to Pylos and Sparta seeking information about Odysseus, a young Ithacan noble made this explanation: "What can one do when such a man, troubled in heart, begs? It would be difficult to refuse the gift." [25] In still another category payment for service was combined with the ceremonialism necessary to an important event. There is much talk in the *Odyssey* about the "gifts of wooing," and the successful suitor, who reminds one of nothing so much as the highest bidder at an auction, in turn received his counter-gift in the dowry, without which there could be no marriage. The whole of what we call foreign relations and diplomacy, in their peaceful manifestations, was conducted by gift-exchange. And even in war occasions presented themselves, as between Diomedes and Glaucus, for example, or Ajax and Hector, when heroes from the two contending sides stopped, right on the field of combat and before the approving eyes of their fellow heroes, and exchanged armor.

Odyssean trade differed from the various forms of gift-exchange in that the exchange of goods was the end itself. In trade things changed hands because each needed what the other had, and not, or only incidentally, to compensate for a service, seal an alliance, or support a friendship. A need for some specific object was the ground for the transaction; if it could be satisfied by other means, trade was altogether unnecessary. Hence, in modern parlance, imports alone motivated trade, never exports. There was never a need to export as such, only the necessity of having the proper goods for the counter-gift when an import was unavoidable.

Laertes bought Eurycleia "with (some of) his possessions . . . , and he gave the worth of twenty oxen." [26] Cattle were the measuring stick of worth; in that respect, and only in that sense, cattle were money. Neither cattle, however, nor anything else served for the various other, later uses of money. Above all, there was no circulating medium like a coin, the sole function of which was to make purchase and sale possible by being passed from hand to hand. Almost any useful object served, and it is noteworthy that the measure of value, cattle, did not itself function as a medium of exchange. Laertes bought Eurycleia for unspecified objects worth twenty oxen; he would never have traded the oxen for a slave.

A conventional measuring stick is no more than an artificial language, a symbol like the X, Y, Z of algebra. By itself it cannot decide how much iron is the equivalent of one cow, or how much wine. In Adam Smith's world that determination was made through the supply-and-demand market, a mechanism utterly unknown in Troy or Ithaca. Behind the market lies the profit motive, and if there was one thing that was taboo in Homeric exchanges it was gain in the exchange. Whether in trade or in any other mutual relationship, the abiding principle was equality and mutual benefit. Gain at the expense of another belonged to a different realm, to warfare and raiding, where it was achieved by acts (or threats) of prowess, not by manipulation and bargaining. Gain from trade was "greedy gain."

The implication that exchange rates were customary and conventional seems unavoidable. That is to say, there was no constituted authority with the power to decree a set of equations —so much of X for so much of Y. Rather the actual practice of exchange over a long period of time had fixed the ratios, and they were commonly known and respected. Even in the distribution of booty, where a central authority, the head of the *oikos* or a king or commander-in-chief, took charge, he was obviously bound by what was generally deemed to be equitable. The circumstance that no one could punish him for flouting custom, as in the conflict between Agamemnon and Achilles, is irrelevant to the issue. For the very fact that just such a situation gave the theme for the *Iliad* illustrates how dangerous the violation could be. In this world custom was as binding upon the individual as the most rigid statutory law of later days. And the participant in an exchange, it may be added, had the advantage over the passive participant in the distribution of booty. He could always refuse to go through with the transaction if the rules were manifestly being upset, or if he merely thought they were.

None of this is to say that no one ever deliberately profited from an exchange. But the exceptional instance is far less noteworthy than the essential point that, in a strict sense, the ethics of the world of Odysseus prohibited the practice of trade as a vocation. The test of what was and what was not acceptable did not lie in the act of trading, but in the status of the trader and in his approach to the transaction. So crucial was the need for metal that even a king could honorably voyage in its search. When Athena appeared to Telemachus as Mentes, the Taphian chieftain, her story was that she was carrying iron to Temesa in quest of copper.* That gave no difficulties, and her visit ended with the colloquy regarding costly gifts between guest-friends.

A stranger with a ship was not always so welcome or so free from suspicion. He might have been Odysseus before Ismarus, or Achilles: "Twelve cities of men have I destroyed from shipboard and eleven on foot, I say, in the fertile region of Troy; from all these I took out much good treasure." [27] No wonder that some Greeks eventually objected to Homer as the teacher of the Hellenes. Glorification of piracy, disapproval of theft (seizure of goods by stealth), and encouragement of robbery (seizure of goods and persons by physical prowess)—truly this seemed a world of mixed-up moral standards. "Theft of property is mean," protested Plato, "seizure by force shameless; none of the sons of Zeus delighted in fraud or violence, nor practiced either. Therefore, let no one be falsely persuaded by poets or by some myth-tellers in these matters." [28]

Yet there was a pattern and a consistency in the moral code; and it made sense from the premises. The distinctions rested on a specific social structure, with strongly entrenched

---

* Neither Taphos nor Temesa is otherwise known as a place name, and the many attempts, all failures, to identify them with one or another mining region illustrate once again the futility of such "historicizing" of the Homeric poems.

notions regarding the proper ways for a man to behave, with respect to property, toward other men. Upon his arrival among the Phaeacians, but before he had identified himself and told of his wanderings, Odysseus was entertained by King Alcinous. Following the feast, the younger nobles competed in athletics. After a time the king's son Laodamas approached Odysseus and invited him to participate.

"Come, stranger and father, you enter the games, if perchance you are skilled in any; you seem to know games. For there is no greater fame for a man, so long as he is alive, than that which is made by foot and hand."

Odysseus asked to be excused, pleading the heavy burden of his sorrows. Another young aristocrat then interposed. "No indeed, stranger, I do not think you are like a man of games, such as there are many among men; but like one who travels with a many-benched ship, a master of sailors who traffic, one who remembers the cargo and is in charge of merchandise and greedy gains." [29]

The insult was unbearable under all circumstances, and to Homer's audience it must have carried an added barb when directed against Odysseus. There was something equivocal about Odysseus as a hero precisely because of his most famed quality, his craftiness. There was even a soft spot in his inheritance: his maternal grandfather, the goodly Autolycus, "surpassed all men in thievishness and the oath, for that was a gift to him from the god Hermes." [30] Later the doubts of many Greeks turned to open contempt and condemnation. "I know full well," says Philoctetes in the Sophoclean play, "that he would attempt with his tongue every evil word and villainy." [31] What saved the Homeric Odysseus was the fact that his guile was employed in the pursuit of heroic goals; hence Hermes, the god of tricks and stealth, may have given him the magic with which to ward off Circe the witch, but it was Athena who was his protector and his inspiration in his heroic exploits. To the insult in Phaeacia he first replied with an indignant speech, but Odysseus, of all men, could not establish his status with words. Having finished his reply, he leaped up, seized a weight greater than any the young men had cast, and, without removing his garment, threw it far beyond their best mark.

Possibly there were men, a very few from among those who were not men of games, living in the interstices of society, who traveled in many-benched ships and trafficked. Yet there is no single word in either the *Iliad* or the *Odyssey* that is in fact a synonym for "merchant." By and large, the provisioning of the Greek world with whatever it obtained from the outside by peaceful means was in the hands of non-Greeks, the Phoenicians in particular. They were really a trading people, who sailed from one end of the known world to the other, carrying slaves, metal, jewelry, and fine cloth. If they were motivated by gain—"famed for ships, greedy men" [32]—that was irrelevant to the Greeks, the passive participants in the operation.

The need for metal, or any similar need, was an *oikos* affair, not an individual matter. Its acquisition, whether by trade or by raid, was therefore a household enterprise, managed by the head. Or it could be larger in scale, involving many households acting cooperatively. Internally, the situation was altogether different. Trade within the household was impossible by definition: the *oikos* was a single, indivisible unit. Because a large sector of the population was enmeshed in the great households, it too was withdrawn from any possibility of trade, external or internal. The *thetes,* finally, were absolutely excluded; having nothing, they had nothing to exchange.

That leaves the non-aristocratic, small-scale herders and peasants. In their households shortages were chronic, if not absolute as a consequence of a crop failure or a disaster to their flocks, then partial because of an imbalance in the yield. Their troubles are not the subject of heroic poetry, and neither the *Iliad* nor the *Odyssey* is informative in this regard. The inference is permissible, however, that some of their difficulties were alleviated by barter, primarily with one another, and without the instrumentality of a market or fair, absolutely unknown in this world. They exchanged necessities, staples, undoubtedly on the same principles of equivalence, ratios fixed by custom, and no gain.

Herders and peasants, including the *thetes,* always had another resource to draw upon. They could work. As with trade, so with labor, the society's moral judgment was directed not to the act itself but to the person and the circumstance. Back in Ithaca, but still disguised as a beggar, Odysseus, in reply to Eurymachus's mocking offer of employment, challenged the suitor to a plowing contest—just as, in his proper guise, he boasted of his superior bowmanship or his weight throwing. But Odysseus was not required to plow in order to live. In fact, it is obvious that, though he knew how to till and herd and build a raft, he rarely did any work on his estate except in sport. That was the great dividing line, between those who were compelled to labor and those who were not. Among the former, the men with the inspired skills, the bards and the metalworkers and the others, were an elite. Above all, the test was this, that "the condition of the free man is that he not live under the constraint of another." [33] Hence there was a sharp line between those who, though they worked, remained their own masters, the independent herders and peasants, and on the other side the *thetes* and the slaves who labored for others, whose livelihood was not in their own hands. The slaves, at least, were usually the victims of chance. The *thes* was in that sense the worst of all: he voluntarily contracted away his control over his own labor, in other words, his true freedom.

Much of the psychology of labor, with its ambivalence between admiration of skill and craft and its rejection of the laborer as essentially and irretrievably an inferior being, found its symbol on Olympus. Having humanized the gods, the bard was consistent enough to include labor among the heavenly pursuits. But that entailed a certain difficulty. Zeus the insatiable philanderer, Apollo the archer who was also a minstrel, Ares the god of battle—these were all embodiments of noble attributes and activities, easily recreated in man's image. But how could the artisan who built their palaces and made their weapons and their plate and their ornaments be placed on equal footing with them, without casting a shadow over the hierarchy of values and status on which society rested? Only a god could make swords for gods, yet somehow he must be a being apart from the other gods.

The solution was neatly turned, very neatly indeed. The divine craftsman was Hephaestus, son of Hera. His skill was truly fabulous, and the poet never tired of it, lingering over his forge and his productions as he never sang of the smith in Ithaca. That was the positive side of the ambivalence. The other was this: of all the gods, Hephaestus alone was "a huge limping monster" with "a sturdy neck and hairy chest." [34] Hephaestus was born lame, and he carried the mark of his

shame on his whole personality. The other gods would have
been less than human, in consequence, were Hephaestus not
to be their perennial source of humor. Once, when Zeus and
Hera were having a fearful quarrel, the limping god attempted
the role of peacemaker, filling the cups with nectar for all the
assemblage. "And unquenchable laughter was stirred up among
the blessed gods as they watched Hephaestus bustling about
the palace." [35] And the social fabric of the world of Odysseus
was saved.

In fact, the mirror-image on Olympus was still more subtle.
In art and craftsmanship, Athena was frequently linked with
Hephaestus, as in the simile in which a comparison is drawn
with a goldsmith, "a skillful man whom Hephaestus and Pallas
Athena taught all kinds of craft (*techne*)." [36] But there was
absolutely nothing deformed or the least bit comical about
Athena, deservedly her father's favorite among the gods. It was
unnecessary to apologize for Athena's skill with her hands, for
the pattern with respect to work differed somewhat for women.
Denied the right to a heroic way of life, to feats of prowess,
competitive games, and leadership in organized activity of any
kind, women worked, regardless of class. With her maids,
Nausicaa, daughter of the Phaeacian king, did the household
laundry. Queen Penelope found in her weaving the trick with
which to hold off the suitors. Her stratagem, however, of undoing at night what she had woven in the day, repeated without detection for three full years until one of her maids revealed
the secret, suggests that her labor was not exactly indispensable.
The women of the aristocracy, like their men, possessed all the
necessary work skills, and they used them more often. Nevertheless, their real role was managerial. The house was their

domain, the cooking and the washing, the cleaning and the clothes-making. The dividing line for them was rather in the degree to which they performed the chores themselves—between those who supervised, working only to pass the time, and those whom circumstances compelled to cook and sew in earnest.

CHAPTER IV

Household, Kin, and Community

The subject of heroic poetry is the hero, and the hero is a man who behaves in certain ways, pursuing specified goals by his personal courage and bravery. The social background is little more than the stage on which the heroes move. No one who reads the *Iliad* can fail to be struck by the peculiar character of the fighting. There are tens of thousands of soldiers on hand, yet the poet has eyes only for Ajax or Achilles or Hector or Aeneas. In itself, such a literary device is commonplace; it is a very rare artist who has both reason and genius enough to recreate masses of men in battle. Nor is there historical objection to the individual combat between champions, as between Achilles and Hector, or, even more interesting in some ways, between Ajax and Hector, ending in a draw and an exchange of gifts. The false note comes in the full-scale fighting. There the confusion is indescribable. No one commands or gives orders. Men enter the battle and leave at their own pleasure; they select their individual opponents; they group and regroup for purely personal reasons. And the disorganization, unlike the chaotic movements in a war novel like *The Red Badge of Courage,* does not stem from the breakdown of an original

74

plan of action, but from the poet's fundamental disinterest in anything but his heroes as individuals. He must bring in the army as a whole to maintain the necessary realism of the background, but he returns to the central figures as quickly as possible. For Stephen Crane the confusion was itself a most important part of his story, for Homer merely an unavoidable condition of heroic poetry.

Off the field of battle there are hundreds of small details essentially irrelevant to either the narrative or the action of the heroes. The hanging of the twelve slave girls, Mentes' cargo of iron, the purchase of Eurycleia by Laertes, Telemachus's visit to the storeroom—these odd bits are too fragmentary to have interest as independent scenes and in a sense they are all unnecessary for the movement of the tale. Yet the poet introduces them on every page, briefly, in a few phrases or lines, but with the greatest skill and attention. Both the artistry of the narrative and the conviction with which it was received rest in large measure on these incidentals. They underscore or elucidate behavior, they give color to the proceedings, and they remind the audience again and again of the truthfulness of the account. And today they have the added function of helping to make accessible a complicated social system and its values.

In the action of the individual heroes, status was perhaps the main conditioning factor; in the first instance, class status. A man's work and the evaluation of his skills, what he did and what he was not to do in the acquisition of goods and their disposition, within the *oikos* and without, were all status-bound. It was a world of multiple standards and values, of diversified permissions and prohibitions. With respect to work and wealth, at least, the determinant was always the particular social grouping to which one belonged, not the skills, desires, or enterprise of an individual. The chief heroes were individuals, not robots. Nevertheless, in all their behavior, by no means in the economic sphere alone, the implicitly indicated limits to tolerable individual initiative and deviance were extremely narrow: among the nobles, only in the degree of one's strength and prowess, the magnitude of one's ambition for glory, and the development of one's sense of what was fitting. There were variations in temperament, too, like Odysseus' outstanding craftiness or Achilles' excessive sensitivity, but they were more puzzling than not.

Agamemnon is a convenient illustration of the far-reaching effects of status. He is several times called "most kingly" of the heroes at Troy, clearly not in sarcasm, yet he was by no means the most heroic in his personal capacities or accomplishments. His position at the head of the invading forces was not personally earned but was the consequence of his superior position in power, as the leader who could bring the largest contingent, one hundred ships. His status gave him command, hence the right to distribute the booty and select the prize of honor. His status also prevented the aggrieved Achilles from expressing defiance other than in the passive form of a mighty sulk, though in valor Achilles was the admitted superior.

Or consider Telemachus. He was still a youngster, to be sure, yet there was unmistakable irritation in Athena's "You ought not continue your childish ways, now that you are no longer of an age." [1] Maturity was more than chronological; a twenty-year-old of such lineage and class was expected to grow faster and further, and to respond sooner to circumstances requiring adult behavior.

Athena was prodding Telemachus hard because of the grave situation created by the suitors. She pointed to Orestes as a model. "Have you not heard what fame illustrious Orestes received among all men when he killed his father's murderer, wily Aegisthus?" * Penelope's suitors had committed no murder, nor were they threatening one (later they tried unsuccessfully to ambush and assassinate Telemachus). Nevertheless, Orestes was a proper model for Odysseus' son, altogether apart from the hero-theme of glory and honor. Both young men faced obligations of the same species, namely, those that stemmed from the family, the one to avenge his father's death, the other to preserve his paternal *oikos*.

Orestes and Aegisthus, Telemachus and all 108 suitors were nobles. Within that single social class, however, there was another kind of group relationship and group loyalty, the family bond. Agamemnon, it may be noted, was supported in his right to lead the Greek armies by the fact that his brother Menelaus was the aggrieved party to be avenged. When criminal acts were involved, the family, not the class (or the community as a whole), was charged with preserving the standards of conduct and with punishing any breach.

Historically there is an inverse relationship between the extension of the notion of crime as an act of public malfeasance and the authority of the kinship group. Many primitive societies are known in which it is not possible to find any "public" responsibility to punish an offender. Either the victim and his relations take vengeance or there is none whatsoever. The growth of the idea of crime, and of criminal law, could almost

* *Odyssey* 1.298–300. Whenever Orestes is mentioned in the *Odyssey* no reference is made to his having also killed his mother Clytaemnestra. Yet that is the central theme of the Orestes tragedy in Greek drama. However one explains Homer's silence, the contrast, and the obviously contemporary matter in the plays, notably the court scenes, indicate once again that information taken from post-Homeric treatment of the old myths is worse than useless in a study of the world of Odysseus. Later poets and playwrights reworked the materials freely, and with total unconcern for history.

be written as the history of the chipping away of that early state
of family omnipotence. The crumbling process had not advanced very far by the time of Orestes and Telemachus, nor
did it begin in the places modern Western man, with his own
peculiar ethical traditions, would surely have selected. Homicide, as the most obvious example, remained largely a private
affair. Much as the collective conscience may have thought
punishment desirable, it failed to provide any instrumentality
outside of the kinsmen. They in turn refused to distinguish
among homicides as between a justified one and a malicious
one. Odysseus' slaughter of the suitors brought their fathers and
relations to arms. "For this is dishonor," said Antinous's father,
"even for those who come after to hear, if we do not avenge the
murder of our sons and brothers." [2] Had Athena not intervened
to close the poem, as she opened it, no human force in Ithaca
could have prevented still more bloodshed.

The profundity of the Greeks' kinship attachment, throughout their history, is immediately apparent from their passion for
genealogies. That never changed radically at any time. The
language of family was altered, however, and the tendency was
toward narrowing the circle. Homer has a special word, *einater*,
for a husband's brother's wife, to cite a clear-cut example, and
that word soon disappeared from the ordinary vocabulary. The
reason for the change is not hard to find. In a household like
Priam's there were many women whose relationship to one another was that of husband's brother's wife. When that kind of
massive family disappeared, when daughters went off to their
husbands' homes and sons set up their own establishments
while the father still lived, the fine distinction of *einater* became
super-fine. The more general word *kedestes* for every in-law
was then good enough.

The coexistence of three distinct but overlapping groups, class, kin, and *oikos,* was what defined a man's life, materially and psychologically. The demands of each of the three did not always coincide; when they conflicted openly there were inevitable tensions and disequilibriums. And then there was still a fourth group in the picture. Once Athena had put a little backbone into Telemachus he, still at her suggestion, summoned the Ithacans to an assembly. The first speaker, an old noble named Aegyptius, asked who had called the meeting and on what business. In reply Telemachus repeated the phrasing of the question in part when he said, "Neither have I heard any news that the army (*i.e.,* Odysseus and his men) is returning . . . nor do I disclose or speak of any other public matter." Then he added, "But of my own matter, for an evil has fallen on my household, a double one." ³

The twin evils were Odysseus' failure to return and the suitors' refusal to clear out. The suitors were altogether Telemachus's private business. But old Aegyptius thought that the meeting had been called on a public matter, and the very existence of such a notion is significant. The assembly (*agora*)* was unknown among the Cyclopes; that was the second item listed by Odysseus as a sign of their wholly uncivilized state (the absence of *themis* was the third).† An assembly is no simple institution. As a precondition it requires a relatively settled, stable community made up of many households and kinship

---

* "Assembly" is the original sense of *agora,* both the place of meeting and the meeting itself. The market-place connotation, with which it is most commonly associated in the modern mind, is very much later. There is not a trace of it in Homer.

† *Themis* is untranslatable. A gift of the gods and a mark of civilized existence, sometimes it means right custom, proper procedure, social order, and sometimes merely the will of the gods (as revealed by an omen, for example) with little of the idea of right.

groups; in other words, the imposition upon kinship of some territorial superstructure. That means that the several households and larger family groups had substituted for physical coexistence at arm's length a measure of common existence, a community, and hence a partial surrender of their own autonomy. In this new and more complex structure of society a private affair was one that remained within the sole authority of the *oikos* or kinship group, a public matter one in which the decision was for the heads of all the separate groups to make, consulting together.

Neither the beginnings nor the early history of the Greek community can be described. The original Greek migrants into the eastern Mediterranean region were not primitive hunters. They were a pastoral people who, so the signs seem to say, had learned the art of agriculture as well. Apparently their organization was tribal, modified by temporary expedients while they were on the move. But the world they entered was far more complex, especially so on its perimeter, where, in Egypt and the Near East, there had already been a long experience in large-scale territorial organization. In the thousand years, roughly, that ensued until the age of Odysseus, social and political organization had a relatively complicated history. There was no standing still for a thousand years; nor was the movement all in a straight line or all in one direction, up or down. These were centuries filled with violent upheavals and catastrophes, leaving clear if not very legible imprints on the archaeological record. When they occurred with sufficient force they brought down institutions along with the stone walls and the lives of men.

Odysseus' Ithaca was more household- and kinship-bound, less integrally a civic community, than many a civilized center of earlier centuries. We are led to the conclusion that the destruction that was nearly universal in the eastern Mediterranean in the period 1200–1100 B.C., whether caused by the Dorian invasion of tradition or by some other force, carried away much of the existing political structure and replaced it by the unbounded kinship principle. There is the further implication, however, that the slow return of the community was no longer a new thing among the heroes of the poems, that *agora* and *themis,* and the idea that there were both public and private matters, were well established in their thinking. The assembled Ithacans were puzzled by several aspects of Telemachus's summons; there is no sign of discomfort or uncertainty in how to go about the business of an assembly.

The rules were rather simple. The assembly was normally summoned by the king at his pleasure, without advance notice. When the men were abroad on a campaign, an assembly could be called in the camp to consider matters pertaining to the war.* At home or in the field there were no stated meeting dates, no fixed number of sessions. In Odysseus' absence, Ithaca had gone more than twenty years without a meeting, yet others were seemingly empowered to call one had they so wished, just as Achilles once assembled the Achaeans in the field although Agamemnon, not he, was commander-in-chief. Aegyptius's query in Ithaca implied no doubt about the validity of the assembly summoned by Telemachus; the old man was merely curious to know who had broken the twenty-year silence.

The usual time of meeting was dawn. "And when rosy-fingered Dawn appeared, the child of morn, the dear son of Odysseus rose from his bed and put on his garments. . . .

---

* At the end of the third century B.C. a meeting of the armed levy of the Aetolian League sometimes functioned as a regular assembly of the League.

Straightway he bade the clear-voiced heralds summon the long-haired Achaeans to an assembly. They made the call, and the latter gathered swiftly indeed." [4] The one item on the agenda was the issue the summoner wanted discussed. Whoever felt moved to speak rose to do so, and while he talked he held the scepter placed in his hand by the herald—in a quite literal sense a magic wand that rendered the speaker physically inviolate. Custom gave the eldest the first opportunity to take the floor. Thereafter the sequence was determined by the course of the debate rather than by a fixed seniority system. And when there were no more speakers the meeting dissolved.

The assembly neither voted nor decided. Its function was twofold: to mobilize the arguments pro and con, and to show the king or field commander how sentiment lay. The sole measure of opinion was by acclamation, not infrequently in less orderly forms, like the shouting down of an unpopular presentation. The king was free to ignore the expression of sentiment and go his own way. That, in fact, was what introduced the theme for the *Iliad*. A priest had come to the Achaean camp to ransom his captive daughter Chryseis. He made a brief plea and "all the other Achaeans assented by acclamation to reverence the priest and to accept the splendid ransom; but it did not please the heart of Atreus's son Agamemnon and roughly he sent him away." [5] In great anger the god Apollo came down from Olympus and for nine days poured arrows into the Achaean host, "and the close-set pyres of the dead burned continuously," until Hera took pity and bade Achilles summon an assembly. There Agamemnon, in a violent quarrel with Achilles, bowed to Apollo, agreed to release the priest's daughter, and then made the personal, unilateral decision to replace her in his hut with Briseis, the prize among Achilles' captives.

Achilles spoke six times at the meeting, Agamemnon four, but throughout they addressed each other directly, like two men wrangling in the privacy of their homes. Once Agamemnon interrupted what he was saying to Achilles, turned to the assemblage, and announced his decision to surrender Chryseis and the procedure to be followed to appease the god. Apart from this one moment, the disputants talked only to each other. When Nestor intervened near the end to urge peace between them, he too spoke only to the two heroes. Finally, "when the two had finished fighting with quarrelsome words, they dissolved the assembly beside the ships of the Achaeans." [6] In this instance, unlike others in the *Iliad,* the army indicated no preference or sentiment of any kind.

Such a performance and so informal an institution as this sort of assembly are not easily evaluated in parliamentary terms. A king or commander-in-chief was under no compulsion to call a meeting, and yet the aristocracy, and in a certain sense even the people, had a right to be heard, for otherwise no one other than the king could have issued a summons. The chief nobles served the king as a council of elders, and again there was nothing binding about their recommendations. On one occasion, for example, King Alcinous assembled the Phaeacian "chieftains and leaders," informed them of his decision to have Odysseus convoyed to Ithaca, and then led him to the feast, without even a pause for their comment or reaction.

Nevertheless the *Iliad* and *Odyssey* are filled with assemblies and discussions, and they were not mere play-acting. Viewed from a narrow conception of formal rights, the king had the power to decide, alone and without consulting anyone. Often he did. But there was *themis*—custom, tradition, folkways, mores, whatever we may call it, the enormous power of "it is (or is not) done." The world of Odysseus had a highly developed sense of what was fitting and proper. Only once in either poem did a commoner, Thersites, presume to take the floor at an assembly, and he was promptly beaten down by Odysseus. Thersites behaved improperly: the people acclaimed or dissented as they listened, they did not themselves make proposals. That was a prerogative of the artistocrats; it was their role to advise, the king's to take heed if he would. "It behooves you," Nestor told Agamemnon at a meeting of the elders, "more than anyone both to speak words and to listen." [7] The king who ignored the prevailing sentiment was within his right, but he ran a risk. Any ruler must calculate on the possibility that those bound by law or custom to obey him may one day refuse, by passive resistance or outright revolt. The Homeric assembly thus served the kings as a test of public opinion, as the council of elders revealed the sentiment among the nobles.

A large measure of informality, of fluidity and flexibility, marked all the political institutions of the age. There were lines of responsibility and power, and they were generally understood, but they often crossed, and then there was trouble. If the king in assembly could ignore its opinion, no matter how clear and unanimous, it was equally true that the Greek world got along as well as ever without kings for ten years—and Ithaca, for twenty. This was possible because the superimposition of a community, the territorial unit under a king, upon the household-kinship system merely weakened the dominant position of the latter, but only in part and only in certain respects. Primarily it was war, defensive in particular, which was an activity of the community, while the usual pursuits of peace, the procurement of sustenance, social intercourse, the administration of justice, relations with the gods, and even non-

bellicose relations with the outside world, were largely conducted, as before, through the interlocking channels of *oikos,*
kin, and class.

And kinship thinking permeated everything. Even the relatively new, non-kinship institutions of the community were
shaped as much as possible in the image of the household and
the family. The perfect symbol, of course, was the metaphor
of the king as father (on Olympus, Zeus was called "father of
the gods," which, taken literally, he was of some but not of
others). In certain of his functions—in the assembly, for example, or in offering sacrifices to the gods—the king in fact
acted the patriarch. The Greek verb *anassein,* which means
"to be a lord," "to rule," is used in the poems for both the
king (*basileus*) and the head of an *oikos* with almost complete
indifference. It is equally applicable to the gods; Zeus, for instance, "rules (*anassein*) over gods and men." [8]

To rule, after all, is to have power, whether over things,
over men (by other men or some god), or over men and
gods together (by Zeus). But the bardic formulas sometimes
add a little touch that is extremely revealing. In five instances
anassein is qualified with the adverb *iphi,* "by might," so that
king's rule (but never the householder's) becomes rule by
might. This must under no circumstances be taken to imply
tyranny, forcible rule in the invidious sense. When Hector
prayed for his son to "rule by might in Ilion," [9] he was asking
the gods that the boy succeed to the throne, not that he be
endowed with the qualities of a despot. And when Agamemnon named one daughter Iphianassa, he was calling her "prin-
cess," just as Iphigenia, "mightily born," indicates royal birth.

Iphi quietly directs attention to the limits upon the parallel
between head of a household and king. One critical test lay

in the succession. The kings, like Hector, were personally interested in pushing the family parallel to the point at which their sons could automatically follow them on the throne as they succeeded them in the *oikos*. "The king is dead! Long live the king!" That proclamation is the final triumph of the dynastic principle in monarchy. But never in the world of Odysseus was it pronounced by the herald. Kingship had not come that far, and the other aristocrats often succeeded in forcing a substitute announcement: "The king is dead! The struggle for the throne is open!" That is how the entire Ithacan theme of the *Odyssey* can be summed up. "Rule by might," in other words, meant that a weak king was not a king, that a king either had the might to rule or he did not rule at all.

In one of his frequent taunting interchanges with the suitors Telemachus spoke rather curiously: "After all, here in sea-girt Ithaca there are many other kings (*basileis*) among the Achaeans, young and old, one of whom may take the place, since illustrious Odysseus is dead." [10] This remark is different from Nestor's calling Agamemnon "most kingly," for there the comparison was with the assembled heroes at Troy, many of whom were in fact kings at home, whereas here Telemachus meant the nobles of Ithaca, not one of whom was a king. Were this a unique passage, it could be ignored as a first crude effort on the part of Telemachus, whose growing-up process had begun on that same day, to imitate the guile of his father. But the oscillation between *basileus* as king and *basileus* as chief— that is, as head of an aristocratic household with its servants and retainers—is duplicated elsewhere in the Homeric poems and by other early writers. Nor is this an instance of poverty of language. Behind the terminology can be felt all the pressure of the aristocracy to reduce kingship to a minimum. Aristocracy was prior to kingship logically, historically, and socially. While recognizing monarchy, the nobles proposed to maintain the fundamental priority of their status, to keep the king on the level of a first among equals.

The fundamental conflict is laid bare in all its complexity in the opening book of the *Odyssey*. Telemachus's reference to the many kings in Ithaca was said in his reply to a challenge by the suitor Antinous: "Never may Cronion (i.e., Zeus) make you king in sea-girt Ithaca, which is your patrimony by birth." Telemachus sadly conceded the probable truth of that hope and prophecy, and went on to demand that his household, as distinct from the kingship, be returned to him. "Telemachus," was the answer of another suitor, the more guileful Eurymachus, "it really lies in the lap of the gods, who shall be king of the Achaeans in sea-girt Ithaca. But may you keep your own property and be lord (*anassein*) in your house." [11] Let Penelope choose Odysseus' successor as king and spouse, and peace would be restored in Ithaca. The successful suitor would take the throne and Telemachus could "with pleasure enjoy all (his) patrimony, eating and drinking, while she attends to the house of another." [12] Otherwise the daily feasting would continue in this curious war of attrition, until one day Telemachus would find himself with no household worth inheriting.

The element of naked force was not at all disguised. Both sides piously left the decision to the gods, but prudence dictated that the immortals be guided in their decision by the power of mortal arms. In the futile assembly that Telemachus summoned on the following day, Leocritus openly and bluntly warned that "if Odysseus of Ithaca himself were to come and were eager in his heart to drive from the palace the noble suitors who feast in his house, yet his wife would find no pleas-

ure in his coming, though she yearns for him. On the contrary,
just there would he meet with evil destiny, were he to fight
against greater numbers." [13]

Leocritus was a poor prophet. But the fact is that when
Odysseus returned there was no automatic resumption of his
royal position. He had to fight against heavy odds and with all
his powers of strength and guile to regain his throne. Leocritus
had overlooked one matter, the interest of Athena in Odysseus.
"I should surely have perished in my palace of the evil fate of
Agamemnon son of Atreus, had not you, goddess, told me
each thing rightly." [14]

It may be protested that all this is to read historical significance into what is no more than the story line of the poem. Had
Odysseus not returned, we should have had no *Odyssey;* had he
met the fate from which the goddess rescued him, we should
have had an altogether different tale. True; but we must remember that Odysseus is our conventional name for King X.
Stripped of the details of myth and narrative, the diversified
homecomings are precisely what would have occurred in this
world, with its delicate, easily upset balance of powers. Nestor
and Menelaus smoothly picked up the threads as they had
been before the expedition, although each in different personal
circumstances; Agamemnon was murdered by Aegisthus, his
successor as spouse, master of the household, and king; Odysseus contrived to avoid that fate, though faced with 108 potential Aegisthuses. Historically and sociologically these tales
simply mean that some kings had established such personal
power and authority that no challenge was possible, that others
were challenged unsuccessfully, and that still others learned that
"first among equals" was no position from which to look for-

ward to a long life of blessings and comforts. Nor was a
Trojan War necessary as the igniting spark, although obviously
such an enforced absence could facilitate the mobilization of
hostile forces.

The uncertainties of kingship may be pursued one step back-
ward in the career of Odysseus. What about Laertes? He was
an old man, indeed, but he was not senile. Why did he not sit
on the throne of Ithaca? Nestor was at least as old—about
seventy in the *Iliad*—and he not only ruled before and after
the war, but accompanied the hosts to Troy; and there, though
his value to the army was only moral and psychological, he was
a leading member of Agamemnon's council of elders. And then
there was old Priam. In the great crisis actual leadership fell
to his son Hector, but Priam was still king beyond dispute.
After Achilles had become reconciled with Agamemnon and
returned to the fray, Aeneas came forward to challenge him to
single combat. Why? asked Achilles. "Does your heart command you to do battle with me in the hope of being master of
Priam's lordship over the horse-taming Trojans? But no, even
though you slay me, Priam will not on that account place the
prerogative in your hands; for he has sons and he is firm and
not weak-minded." [15]

Nor is there a hint that Odysseus had usurped his father's
position; on the contrary, much of the final book of the poem
is given over to a scene of love and devotion between father
and son. Yet so far was the ex-king from authority that all the
while the suitors were threatening to destroy the very substance
of his son and grandson, Laertes could do no more than withdraw in isolation to his farm, there to grieve and lament. Nobles
lived in the town, not on their estates. Laertes, however, "no

longer comes to the town, but far off in the fields suffers misery, with an old woman as attendant, who serves him meat and drink whenever weariness takes hold of his limbs as he drags along the high ground of his vineyard." *

It is idle to guess the circumstances which brought Odysseus to the throne in place of Laertes. The statement must suffice that long before the days when he could only drag himself in his vineyard Laertes had proved unable to rule *iphi,* by might. And so, somehow, the rule passed to his son. In a sense, what modern kings have called the principle of legitimacy was thereby preserved, the same principle which Achilles enunciated for Aeneas, and which he defended for his father Peleus and himself among his Myrmidons. That was Achilles' first concern in Hades when Odysseus paid his call. "Tell me of excellent Peleus, if you have heard anything." Does he still hold his rightful place or has he been pushed aside "because old age has him by hand and foot?" For "I am no longer his aid beneath the rays of the sun," protecting our rule with my might.[16]

In Ithaca not even the arrogant suitors, for all their open threats of violence, could altogether overlook the family claim to the throne. On the surface there is no good reason why they went on with the game for so many years. If force had been the only factor, Leocritus spoke truly when he said they outnumbered any possible opposition; indeed, there was no visible opposition. Yet not only did they refrain from murdering Laertes and Telemachus and seizing power (although they

* *Odyssey* 1.189–93. Note must be taken that a far less pathetic description appears elsewhere in the *Odyssey,* especially in the last book, usually considered to have been composed relatively late: "the fine and well-tilled farm of Laertes. . . . There was his house, and around it ran many huts on every side, in which the trusty slaves ate and sat and slept, who worked at his pleasure" (24.205–10). It is in this book, too, that we have the only explicit reference to Laertes' ever having been king.

did plot at the last minute to assassinate the latter), not only did they publicly and repeatedly concede Telemachus's claim to his *oikos,* but they placed the decision in the strangest place imaginable, in the hands of a woman. There was nothing about the woman Penelope, either in beauty or wisdom or spirit, that could have won her this unprecedented and unwanted right of decision as a purely personal triumph. Institutionally, further-more, this was a solidly patriarchal society, in which even a Telemachus could bid his mother leave the banquet hall and retire to her proper, womanly tasks.[17]

Why this power was given to Penelope is not explained by the poet, and, in fact, he is neither clear nor quite consistent about the legal picture. As his father's heir Telemachus ob-viously had a measure of authority, and Athena pointed to one way out. "As for your mother, if her heart is stirred up to be married, let her return to the palace of her father great in might. They will arrange the wedding feast and array the many gifts, all that should go with a beloved daughter." [18] At the assembly on the next day both Antinous and Eurymachus gave him the same advice, the latter in the very words Athena had used. But "wise" Telemachus demurred. "It is bad for me to repay a large amount to Icarius (Penelope's father), should I myself send my mother back." [19] The "large amount" was the dowry, which had to be restored under such circumstances.

Early in the feast at which Odysseus suddenly revealed him-self and slaughtered the suitors, Telemachus made a remark to one of them which again indicated his authority, but in a differ-ent direction. "I do not hinder the marriage of my mother; instead, I bid her marry whom she wishes and I also (offer to) give countless gifts. I am ashamed to drive her from the palace, against her will, by a word of compulsion." [20] But if Telemachus had the right to order his mother about in the matter of her marriage, either by sending her back to her father or by compelling (or preventing) her choice from among the wooers, how are we to explain, as fact or as law, Athena's rushing to Sparta, where Telemachus was visiting Menelaus, and warning him to return at once? "For her (Penelope's) father and brother," said the goddess, "are now bidding her marry Eurymachus, for he outdoes all the suitors in gifts and he has greatly increased his gifts of wooing." [21]

Perhaps the Penelope situation became so muddled in the long prehistory of the *Odyssey* that the actual social and legal situation is no longer recoverable. Some scholars have seen in it a confused vestige of a mother-right system that prevailed among the Greeks centuries before. They find similar traces in Phaeacia, and indeed the poet uses some very strange language about Queen Arete, niece and consort of Alcinous the king, even to underscoring her "good wits" and her skill in resolving quarrels among men. [22] When you enter the palace, Nausicaa advised Odysseus, pass by my father's throne and go directly to my mother and appeal to her. "If she should be kindly disposed to you in her heart, then there is hope that you will see your friends, and come to your home good to dwell in, and to your native land." [23] Both Arete and Alcinous were kindly disposed, it turned out, and Odysseus was welcomed beyond measure. After he had related many of his adventures, the queen, who was a full participant in the feasting, contrary to all the rules of Greek society of the time, called upon the nobles to supply gifts of treasure. "He is my guest-friend, though each of you shares in the honor." [24] Not even Clytaemnestra would have talked that way, though she was not beyond joining in the plot to murder Agamemnon her lord.

One old Phaeacian noble promptly told Arete that though her proposal was sound—"on Alcinous here depend deed and word." [25] Nausicaa too, before she counseled Odysseus to seek out Arete, identified herself as the "daughter of great-hearted Alcinous, on whom depend the force and the might of the Phaeacians." [26] And throughout the very long Phaeacian section of the poem Alcinous repeatedly exercised unmistakable and unchallenged royal authority. There are other difficulties and apparent contradictions in this section, and it may well be that two conflicting Phaeacian stories were joined in an imperfect composite. But that a repressed memory of ancient matriarchy is reflected in some of the verses seems a fragile argument. Neither Arete nor Penelope met the genealogical requirements of matriarchy: Arete was the daughter of Alcinous's elder brother; Penelope and Odysseus had no blood kinship at all.*

Whatever the explanation for Penelope's sudden acquisition of so puzzling a power of decision, in the end the essential fact is that "as many of the nobles as have power in the islands, in Dulichion and Same and wooded Zacynthus, and as many as are lords in rocky Ithaca" [27]—in short, virtually the whole aristocracy in and around Ithaca—were agreed that the house of Odysseus was to be dethroned. Along with the rule, his successor was also to take his wife, his widow as they thought. On this point they were terribly insistent, and it may be suggested that their reasoning was this: that by Penelope's receiving the suitor of her choice into the bed of Odysseus, some shadow of legitimacy, however dim and fictitious, would be thrown over the new king. In his first speech to the assembly Telemachus had said that the wooers "shrink from going to the house of her

* Among the matriarchal Iroquois, for example, the successor to a deceased chieftain was chosen by the matron of his maternal family.

father Icarius, so that he might marry off his daughter and give her to whomsoever he chooses." [28] Icarius would, of course, have chosen the highest bidder, the one who gave the most valuable gifts of wooing. Yet the suitors' unwillingness to follow this accepted procedure was surely more than niggardliness. If Icarius were to select Penelope's next husband, the successful bidder would acquire a wife but not the kingdom. Rule in Ithaca was not for Icarius, an outsider, to bestow. That prerogative mysteriously belonged to Penelope.

And Penelope was their undoing. On instruction from Athena, she tricked the suitors into letting the returned hero, still in his beggarly disguise, get the great bow into his hands, which none but he could wield, and with it, supported by Telemachus and two slaves, Philoetius and Eumaeus, he slew the interlopers. Once again the narrative detail points to an essential element of Odyssean life: to regain his throne the king could count on no one but his wife, his son, and his faithful slaves; in other words, royal power was personal power. Nothing could be more misleading than the analogy of king against barons at the close of the Middle Ages, in which the ultimate triumph of the royal principle rested on the backing of commoners. In war the commoners of Ithaca or Sparta or Argos took up arms; then, in the face of the hostile outsider, the community was real and meaningful, and the king, as its head and representative, received support and obedience. In peace he was entitled to various perquisites, and under ordinary circumstances they were given freely. But when the lords fell out among themselves the issue was usually one for themselves alone.

Despite the general silence of the poems on the doings of the ordinary people of Greece, there is direct evidence on this score. Toward the close of the assembly summoned by Telem-

achus, Mentor complained: "Now, indeed, I am angry with
the rest of the people (*demos*), as you all sit in silence and do
not upbraid the suitors and keep them in check, they being few
and you many." [29] At the end of the tale, when the suitors were
dead and Odysseus and his father were having their little feast of
reunion at the old man's farm, there was another gathering in
the *agora*. This was the meeting of the irate relatives of the victims, demanding blood vengeance. But it was no formal assembly. The men came together because "Rumor the messenger
went about the city" with the news of the slaughter [30]—Rumor,
who was Zeus's messenger but had never been designated a herald in Ithaca. The poet makes it clear that this was a meeting of
aristocrats (if there were commoners present, they came as retainers of noble households, not as members of the community
of Ithaca). Hence here he never uses such words as *demos* or
"multitude," although some translators have mistakenly injected "the people" into the lines.

The blood-feud rally was normal. Odysseus had himself anticipated such an action when he said to Telemachus after the
slaughter of the suitors: "Let us consider, that all may be for
the very best. For a person who kills but one man in a country
—even one for whom there are not many left behind to help—
flees, forsaking his kinsmen and his fatherland. And we have
killed the pillars of the city, the very noblest of the youths in
Ithaca." [31] This was private vengeance. But what was the point,
at the beginning of the poem, in calling an assembly to consider
what Telemachus explicitly labeled a private matter? Throughout that meeting Telemachus never once addressed the people.
He talked to the suitors, repeating in public what he had already demanded of them in private, that they give up their
improper method of wooing. Only at the end did Mentor turn

to the *demos* and say: I am angry with you that you do not intervene. Telemachus had clearly failed in his purpose, which was to try to mobilize public opinion against the suitors, thus transforming a private matter into a public one, in effect. Realizing this, Mentor brought the issue into the open, again without success. That is why Leocritus could answer with a sneer, "It is difficult to fight against greater numbers about a feast." [32] Mentor had stressed the potential power of the *demos:* "they (the suitors) being few and you many." Oh no, replied Leocritus, the many are disinterested and neutral, and therefore we and our kinsmen and retainers outnumber you and the forces you can muster. Odysseus himself would "meet with evil destiny, were he to fight against greater numbers." [33]

Neutrality is a state of mind, and anyone who enters the arena to fight for power must keep his eyes and ears on the audience; their attitude may shift suddenly, and they may swarm into the pit and take sides. After the plan to ambush Telemachus had failed, Antinous argued with the other suitors that further delay was perilous. Let us take him into the fields, Antinous proposed, and do away with him, for "the multitude no longer bears good will to us in all respects. Come, therefore, before he calls the Achaeans together to an assembly" and tells them how we plotted against his life. "Hearing of these evil deeds, they will not approve. Beware, then, lest they do us evil and drive us from our land, and we come to the country of others." [34]

Antinous feared that the *demos,* previously unmoved by Telemachus's appeal, might now decide to take sides. Notably there was no reference to rights in his speech. It was not the assertion of popular rights that he foresaw, but Telemachus's rapid coming of age, his beginning to rule by might, and hence the danger that he could persuade the *demos* out of its neutrality and into direct action. Perhaps the memory was still with Antinous of the day when his father had fled to Odysseus for asylum from the *demos,* "for they were terribly angry because he had gone off with the Taphian pirates to raid the Thesprotians, who were in friendly relations with us." [35]

Hypothetically, at least, the opposite possibility was also conceivable—that the people would shift to the position of the suitors. When Telemachus was Nestor's guest, Nestor asked him point blank why he continued to suffer the suitors. "Tell me, do you yield willingly or do the people hate you up and down the land, obeying the voice of a god?" [36] Telemachus made no direct reply then, but he was asked the identical question on another occasion, this time by Odysseus in beggarly disguise,[37] and he said that the answer was no to both alternatives. Lack of power alone caused his passivity.

In fact, we are never told what the *demos* of Ithaca really thought about the whole affair. The narrative reached its end without their intervention on either side, despite all the questioning, the doubts and the fears, the efforts to influence public opinion. Like Eliot's women of Canterbury, the *demos* of Ithaca seemed to say by its neutrality:

> Kings rule or barons rule;
>
> .   .   .   .   .
>
> But mostly we are left to our own devices,
> And we are content if we are left alone.

The suitors failed to take up Antinous's proposal that they seek a solution by murdering Telemachus. Whether his fears were warranted or not is unanswerable, for another ending was already prepared. While the conference was going on, Odysseus was hiding in Ithaca, and the suitors were soon to meet death at his hands. What, we may speculate, would have happened had a chance arrow brought Odysseus down at that moment? It does not necessarily follow that the *demos* would have been moved to reprisal. Nothing in the accepted rules of behavior, neither divine precept nor convention, demanded that they act. Homicide was no crime in a public sense, and regicide was but a special kind of homicide. Had Odysseus been killed, Telemachus would have faced a choice: he could play Hamlet or he could play Orestes. That was his familial responsibility; the community had none. "And of the son of Atreus even you have heard, though far off," Nestor had said to Telemachus; "how he came and how Aegisthus devised his evil end. But sadly indeed did he pay for it. How good it is that a son of the dead man should be left, as that son took vengeance on wily Aegisthus, his father's murderer." [38] Telemachus's misfortune was that, faced not with a single enemy but with one hundred and eight, he came from a line of only sons and had no blood-brothers upon whom to call.

Blood vengeance is but the most dramatic indicator that in the world of Odysseus personal power meant the strength of the household and the family. In that sense the personalization of kingly power went very deep. The suitors may have denied any hostile intentions against the *oikos* of Odysseus, but this was an atypical situation in every respect, and Antinous finally suggested that they kill Telemachus and divide the estate among themselves. The rule was complete identity between king's treasury and king's *oikos,* precisely as his personal retainers were his public officials. The gold and bronze and grain and wine and fine cloth that Telemachus saw lying in the locked storeroom belonged to his father and would come to him by inheritance, whether they had been acquired by Odysseus as king or by Odysseus as mere nobleman. No wonder Telemachus said with charmingly naïve pathos, when it seemed that the suitors must surely triumph, "For indeed it is no bad thing to be a king: forthwith his house becomes wealthy and he himself most honored." [39]

The base of royal wealth and power lay in the holdings in land and cattle, without which no man could have become king in the first place. While the king reigned he also had the use of a separate estate, called a *temenos*, which the community placed at his disposal.* This was the sole exception to the rule that all royal possessions and acquisitions melted into his private *oikos*. Next on the list of "royal revenues" came booty—an all-embracing word covering cattle, metal, female captives, and whatever else of wealth was seizable (except land, for the simple reason that wars were not fought for territory and did not lead to its acquisition). In his guise as a Cretan beggar Odysseus boasted to Eumaeus of his former glory. "Nine times did I lead men and fleet ships against men of another land, and very much (booty) fell to me, of which I chose what suited me, and much I then obtained by lot." [40] The ruler thus not only shared with his men in the general distribution of the spoils, equalized by the drawing of lots, but he received an added share, by first choice. In a major expedition the commander-in-chief took the royal share, though other kings were among his followers. "My hands bear the brunt of furious battle; but when the distribution comes your prerogatives are far greater, and I go to my ships bearing something slight, but dear to me, when I am weary of fighting." [41] So Achilles to Agamemnon, and

* The same word was applied to a temple estate set aside for the enjoyment of a god. With the decay of kingship in post-Homeric Greece, the latter became the sole meaning of *temenos*.

though "something slight" underrates somewhat the acquisitions of the "sacker of cities," there is no mistaking the measure of his resentment against Agamemnon, his inferior in prowess but his superior, by right of position, in the sharing of the fruits.

And then there were the gifts, endlessly given and endlessly talked about. No word immediately denoting compulsion, like "taxes" or even feudal "dues," is to be found in the poems for payments from people to ruler, apart from the context of the special prerogative in the distribution of booty and of the meat of sacrificial animals. "And seven well situated cities will I give him . . . ," said Agamemnon. "And there dwell men of many flocks and many herds, who will honor him like a god with gifts." * Details of this gift-giving by the people are utterly lacking; for Ithaca it is not even mentioned. That it took its place, however, alongside booty as an important and continuing reason why it was "no bad thing to be a king" can scarcely be doubted.

At times the gifts, like the benevolences of Charles I, seem something less than voluntary. "Come now," said King Alcinous of the Phaeacians to the nobles feasting the parting Odysseus, "let us each give him a great tripod and a caldron; and we in turn shall gather among the people and be recompensed, for it is burdensome for one person to give without recompense." [42] Nevertheless, it would be a false appreciation to see nothing but euphemism in the insistence on calling such payments "gifts." For one thing, they lacked the regularity of taxes or dues as well as their fixity of amount. Even so limited a play of free choice as the time and amount of the payment

* *Iliad* 9.149–55. Agamemnon's long description of his proposed gift of amends to Achilles is repeated to Achilles by Odysseus, word for word, 9.264–98; the passage quoted here is found in lines 291–97. Agamemnon's right of disposal over seven cities is a unique and unexplained instance in the poems.

gave it overtones of sentiment and value ordinarily absent from taxation. It is difficult to measure this psychological distinction, but it cannot be ignored for that reason. "Honor him like a god with gifts." Fear the gods as one may, they are not tax collectors, and man's relationship to them is of another order. In the same way, a gift to a ruler, even when compulsory for all practical purposes, is in its formal voluntarism of another order from the fixed tax with its openly coercive character.

What was the counter-gift to the people? The answer is chiefly in the area we label foreign affairs. The effective, powerful king gave protection and defense, by his dealings with kings abroad, by his organization of such activities as the building of walls, and by his personal leadership in battle. He was "shepherd of the people," a Homeric commonplace that had none of the Arcadian image in it, only Goethe's "he who is no warrior can be no shepherd." [43] Sarpedon, commander of the Lycian contingent supporting the Trojans, made the point bluntly: "Glaucus, why are we two the most honored in Lycia in seats of honor and meat and full goblets, and all look upon us as gods, and we hold a great *temenos* on the banks of the Xanthus, a fine one of orchard-land and wheat-bearing land? Therefore we must now stand in the first ranks of the Lycians and participate in fiery battle, so that some of the Lycians armed with stout cuirasses may say, 'Our kings who are lords in Lycia are indeed not inglorious, they that eat fat sheep and choice honey-sweet wine; oh no, they are also of stout might, since they fight in the first ranks of the Lycians.' " [44]

The king gave military leadership and protection, and he gave little else, despite some hints of royal justice (and injustice) scattered through the *Odyssey,* once in a lengthier green-pastures simile: "O lady (Penelope), no one among mortal men throughout the boundless earth would blame you, for your fame reaches the wide heaven, as does (the fame) of an excellent king, one who, god-fearing and ruling among men many and mighty, upholds righteousness, and the dark earth bears wheat and barley, and the trees are heavy with fruit, and the flocks bear without fail, and the sea gives forth fish, out of (his) good leadership, and the people thrive under him." [45] This direct linking of right rule and the fruitfulness of nature is anachronistic, as is the notion of "god-fearing"; they belong not to the time of Odysseus but to the seventh century B.C., when the idea of a world ordered by divine justice had entered the minds of men. They belong in the poems of Hesiod, not in the *Odyssey*. Everything that Homer tells us demonstrates that here he permitted a contemporary note to enter, carefully restricting it, however, to a harmless simile and thus avoiding any possible contradiction in the narrative itself. The return of Odysseus to the throne of Ithaca was just and proper, but it was a matter of private action for personal interests, not the triumph of righteousness in the public interest.

One need scarcely ask why Alcinous did not have the people make a direct gift to Odysseus. Tripods and caldrons were treasure, things which only the aristocracy possessed in significant quantity. Nor would it have been fitting to have the common people provide the gifts to speed a hero on his journey. In a society so status-bound, in which gift-giving had a quality of ceremonialism about it, just anyone could not give a gift to anyone else. There were rather strict lines of giving, and grades and ranks of objects. Stated in other terms, the gift and the relationship between giver and recipient were inseparable. What went up the line from the people to their lord was one matter; what went to an outsider was something else again, and no confusion between the two was permissible.

However the psychologists understand the affective side of this gift-giving, functionally it took its place with marriage and with armed might as an act through which status relations were created, and what we would call political obligations. The world of Odysseus was split into many communities more or less like Ithaca. Among them, between each community and every other one, the normal relationship was one of hostility, at times passive, in a kind of armed truce, and at times active and bellicose. When the slaughtered suitors entered Hades, the arrival en masse of the "best men" of Ithaca was startling, and automatically it was attributed to one of two causes. "Did Poseidon," asked the shade of Agamemnon, "stir up heavy winds and high waves and overpower you in your ships? Or did hostile men slay you on dry land while you were rustling cattle and fair flocks of sheep, or while they were defending their city and their women?" *

In so permanently hostile an environment the heroes were permitted to seek allies; their code of honor did not demand that they stand alone against the world. But there was nothing in their social system that created the possibility for two communities, as such, to enter an alliance. Only personal devices were available, through the channels of household and kin. The first of these was marriage, which served, among other things, to establish new lines of kin, and hence of mutual obligation, that crossed and crisscrossed the Hellenic world. Only men arranged marriages, and only a man from whom Zeus had taken the wits would have neglected considerations of wealth, power, and support in making his selection.

Several generations of such calculated dealing out of daugh-

* *Odyssey* 24.109–13. In the earlier scene in Hades, Odysseus greeted the shade of Agamemnon with the identical words (11.399–403).

ters and assorted female relatives created an intricate, and
sometimes confusing, network of obligations. That was one
reason why the heroes memorized their genealogies carefully
and recited them often. When Diomedes and Glaucus "came together in the middle between the two (armies), eager to do
battle," the former stopped and asked a question. "Who are
you, brave sir, of mortal men? For never before have I seen
you in glorious battle." Glaucus's reply was a long recital, full
sixty-five lines, chiefly of the heroic exploits and the begettings
of his grandfather Bellerophon. His final words were: "Of this
lineage and blood I vaunt myself to be."

"So said he," the poet went on, "and Diomedes of the brave
war-cry rejoiced. . . . 'In truth, you are my paternal guest-
friend of old; for illustrious Oineus at one time entertained excellent Bellerophon in his palace and for twenty days he kept
him, and they gave each other fine gifts of guest-friendship.
. . . Therefore I am now a dear guest-friend to you in central
Argos, and you (to me) in Lycia whenever I come to your land.
So let us avoid each other's spears ' "—there are Trojans enough
for me to kill, and Greeks for you. " 'Let us exchange armor
with each other, so that they too may know that we avow our-
selves to be paternal guest-friends.' " [46] (And then it was that
Glaucus went witless and gave golden armor for bronze.)

This is not comic opera. Homer was no Shaw, Diomedes no
chocolate soldier. Guest-friendship was a very serious institution, the alternative to marriage in forging bonds between
rulers; and there could have been no more dramatic test of
its value in holding the network of relationships together than
just such a critical moment. Guest-friend and guest-friendship
were far more than sentimental terms of human affection. In
the world of Odysseus they were technical names for very con-

crete relationships, as formal and as evocative of rights and duties as marriage. And they remained so well thereafter: Herodotus tells how, in the middle of the sixth century before Christ, Croesus, king of Lydia, "sent messengers to Sparta bearing gifts and requesting an alliance." The Spartans "rejoiced at the coming of the Lydians and they took the oaths of guest-friendship and alliance." [47]

The Herodotus story documents the persistence of guest-friendship; it also shows how far the Greek world had moved from the days of Odysseus. Croesus exchanged oaths of guest-friendship with the Spartans, but Homer knew of no such tie between Argives and Lycians or Taphians and Ithacans—only between individuals, Diomedes and Glaucus, "Mentes" and Telemachus. "Guest-friend," it is understood, is the conventional, admittedly clumsy, English rendition of the Greek *xenos* in one of its senses. The same Greek word meant "stranger," "foreigner," and sometimes "host," a confusion symbolic of the ambivalence which characterized all dealings with the stranger in that archaic world.

The first thing we are told about the Phaeacians—immediately establishing the Utopianism of the tale—is that they existed in almost complete isolation; in fact, that Alcinous's father, Nausithous, had transplanted the community from Hypereia to Scheria (both mythical places) to that very end. There is no cause to fear, Nausicaa reassured her maids as they ran from Odysseus on the beach. "That mortal man does not exist, neither has he been born, who comes to the land of the Phaeacians bringing war, for we are very dear to the immortals. We live far off, surrounded by the stormy sea, the outermost of men, and no other mortals have dealings with us." [48] Nausicaa overstated the situation a little. After she had escorted Odysseus to the town, Athena took over and threw a covering of mist about him to ensure his safe arrival at the palace. "Neither look at any man," was the goddess's warning, "nor inquire of one. For they do not readily bear with strangers." [49]

That was one pole: fear, suspicion, distrust of the stranger. With it went his rightlessness, his lack of kin to safeguard or avenge him, as the case may have been, against ill-doing. At the other pole was the general human obligation of hospitality: in one of his attributes the father of the immortals was Zeus Xenios, the god of hospitality. It was precisely in Phaeacia that, after the earlier forebodings, Odysseus was welcomed so richly that King Alcinous and his court became proverbial among later Greeks for their luxurious living. That paradox was a model of the basic ambivalence of the heroic world toward the uninvited stranger, of the rapid oscillation between deep, well-warranted fear and lavish entertainment.

The poet underscores his point in another way among the Cyclopes, again in Never-Never Land. Odysseus' opening gambit was to plead for the traditional hospitality, and Polyphemus replied with the most open cynicism: I shall devour you last among your company; "that shall be my gift of hospitality." [50] Polyphemus stood at one pole only; there was nothing confusing or uncertain about his unmitigated hostility to all strangers. And again Homer had caught the right shading. We, said the Cyclops, "pay no heed to aegis-bearing Zeus, nor to the blessed gods, inasmuch as we are far better." [51] The giant was to pay for his *hybris* soon enough, tricked by the superior craftiness of god-fearing Odysseus. Behind the fairy tale, clearly, there lay a distinct view of social evolution. In primitive times, the poet seems to be suggesting, man lived in a state of permanent struggle and war to the death against the outsider. Then the gods intervened, and through their precepts, their *themis,* a new ideal was set before man, and especially before a king, an obligation of hospitality: "all strangers and beggars are from Zeus." [52] Henceforth men had to pick a difficult path between the two, between the reality of a society in which the stranger was still a problem and a threat, and the newer morality, according to which he was somehow covered by the aegis of Zeus.

Institutionally it was guest-friendship above all that weakened the tension between the poles. Trade may have removed the enmity from the surface for a moment, but it made no lasting contribution in this area. On the contrary, trade tended to strengthen suspicion of the outsider, for all its indispensability. The unrelieved, totally negative Homeric image of the Phoenicians makes that absolutely clear. Once again the point is driven home in Utopia. The Phaeacians were the ideal seamen, men who, unlike the Greeks themselves, had no horror of the sea and no reason to dread it. "For the Phaeacians have no pilots and no rudders, which other ships have; but (the ships) themselves understand the thoughts and intents of men." [53] Yet not only is there no single reference to Phaeacian trade, but it was in Phaeacia that Odysseus received the crowning insult of being likened to a merchant.

Guest-friendship was of an altogether different order and conception. The stranger who had a *xenos* in a foreign land —and every other community was foreign soil—had an effective substitute for kinsmen, a protector, representative, and ally. He had a refuge if he were forced to flee his home, a storehouse on which to draw when compelled to travel, and a source of men and arms if drawn into battle. These were all personal relations, but with the powerful lords the personal merged into the political, and then guest-friendship was the Homeric version, or forerunner, of political and military alliances. Not that every guest-friend automatically and invariably responded to a call to arms; that would have been a pattern of uniformity unattained, and unattainable, in the fluid and unstable political situation of the world of Odysseus. In this respect a guest-friend was like a king; his worth was in direct proportion to his power. During the years of his unexplained absence, all of Odysseus' *xenoi* might well have agreed with his father Laertes when he said to one, "the countless gifts which you gave, you bestowed in vain." [54]

As the suitors entered Hades, Agamemnon's shade addressed Amphimedon in particular. "Do you not remember the time when I came to your house there (in Ithaca) with godlike Menelaus, to urge Odysseus to go along with me to Ilion in the well-benched ships? And it was a whole month before we had sailed across the wide sea, for it was with difficulty that we prevailed upon Odysseus sacker of cities." * To recruit an army among outsiders in what was, to begin with, only a family feud over a stolen wife, Agamemnon naturally made the fullest use of his guest-friends. But having called upon Amphimedon for the service of hospitality, Agamemnon apparently did not ask for his military services. For that he went to Odysseus, the king, with whom he had no formal relationship.

It would be an idle game to try to guess why Amphimedon stayed at home. Or why Odysseus, having finally been prevailed upon and having raised an army, did not, or could not, engage a larger proportion of the Ithacan nobility in the expedition. The fact is that we are left in rather complete darkness about

* *Odyssey* 24.115–19. Presumably it was to Amphimedon's father, Melaneus, that Agamemnon came, for Amphimedon would have been a child then. In what follows I continue to refer to Amphimedon for convenience.

the way the Achaean army was put together. Perhaps the procedure in Ithaca was the same as among Achilles' Myrmidons.
There one son from each family was chosen by lot.[55] More
likely the methods varied from community to community, according to the desires, interests, and, above all, powers of the
respective kings and nobles. No Greek community had been
attacked or even threatened; hence participation in the Trojan
War was of no direct concern to the *demos*.

Again we are reminded of the fluidity of the political scene.
Agamemnon, the most powerful of the many rulers among the
Hellenes, had as his guest-friend in Ithaca not the king, Odysseus, but one of the non-ruling aristocrats, Amphimedon. There
was nothing strange or rare about this. It was repeated all over
the Greek world, just as marriage, rigidly bound within class
lines, was perfectly acceptable between king or king's son and
the daughter of a noble who was not a king. "First among
equals" meant equality of status with respect to the two peaceful relationships that could be established across community
lines, marriage and guest-friendship. There could be no notion
of blood royal in a world in which "there are many other kings"
in each community.

A third kind of relationship existed, however, in which in-
equality was expressed—that of the retainer. While marriage
and guest-friendship went outside the community—the latter
always, the former sometimes—retainership was a strictly internal institution, one that set up a loose hierarchy among the
nobles of a community and played a key role in the internal
power structure. The situation may be stated in another way:
the retainers constituted the third essential element of the aristocratic household, the other two being the members of the family
and the labor force (whether slaves or hirelings). "Retainer" is

a loose word, and that is why it fits the Greek *therapon*. At one end of the scale it defines the free but surely not aristocratic attendants at the palace banquets, who performed the offices "whereby inferiors serve their betters." [56] And at the other end is a hero like Meriones, *therapon* of King Idomeneus of Crete. Meriones enjoys some of the proudest epithets in the poems, such as "the equal of fleet Ares" or "leader of men"; [57] he is one of the very few secondary chieftains named in the catalogue of ships; and his battle prowess receives many lines in the *Iliad*. Nevertheless it must be assumed that Meriones, as a *therapon*, followed Idomeneus to Troy as a matter of obligation, not because he had been "prevailed upon."

Obligations of this nature and intensity, like the obligations imposed by lineage, were personal. That does not mean that they were arbitrary, weak, or uncertain, but it does mean that in very large measure they stood apart from and outside the bonds of community; or better, that they stood above. It was Menelaus who was aggrieved by the flight of Helen, not Sparta. It was his brother Agamemnon who assumed leadership of the war of reprisal, not Mycenae. It was Amphimedon and Odysseus to whom Agamemnon appealed for assistance, not Ithaca. But it was all of Troy that fought back, not out of loyalty to Paris—or even to old Priam, who was bound to uphold his son —but because the Greek invaders threatened to destroy them all.

The ceaseless interplay of household, kin, and community, at home and abroad, created a complex variety of individual situations and difficulties. Yet there was a kind of fundamental pattern, and a trend which, though not really discernible in the poems themselves, can be seen through that most useful of all the instruments of the historian, hindsight. The anthro-

pologists have taught us what a kinship society looks like in its
purer forms. It is characteristic of much of the primitive world
that "the conduct of individuals to one another is very largely
regulated on the basis of kinship, this being brought about by
the formation of fixed patterns of behavior for each recognized
kind of kinship relation." [58] This is no description of the world
of Odysseus, in which the family tie, though strong, was nar-
rowly defined, and in which other strong and often more binding relationships were established outside the blood group. In
evolutionary terms, insofar as they may legitimately be employed, the world of the Homeric poems had advanced beyond
the primitive. Kinship was then but one of several organizing
principles, and not the most powerful one. Pre-eminence lay
in the *oikos,* the large noble household with its staff of slaves
and commoners, its aristocratic retainers, and its allies among
relatives and guest-friends.

Within the household, as within a lineage, the behavior patterns of man to man (and to woman) were graded and fixed.
As between households too, there were many customary rules
of what was proper and what was not, and we must believe
that in the daily routine of life they were obeyed as a matter
of course. But a higher coercive power was largely lacking,
the community principle being still so rudimentary. Therefore,
as one princely *oikos* vied with another for greater wealth and
power, for more prestige and a superior status, breaches of the
rules were common enough to create the almost unbroken tension that was the stamp of heroic existence. In time to come
great moral teachers would make much of this conflict between
status, prestige, and power on the one side and divine *themis*
on the other. Neither the heroes nor their minstrels were systematic thinkers. Moral principles and philosophical abstractions

were no doubt inherent in their tales, but the bards were content simply to tell the story.

"It is no bad thing to be a king," said one of the characters in the story. Yet one need only turn the pages of Homer or read at random in the legends of the Greeks to discover that betrayal and assassination were a most common fate among rulers. Olympian Zeus himself had become chief of the gods only by overthrowing his father Cronus and the other Titans, and Cronus before him found the path to power equally bloody. One may assess the meaning of the myth-symbols as one wishes. One may allow for the fact that narrative poetry is poetry of action, and that before the invention of romantic love deeds of violence made up the whole of the thematic material. Nevertheless it is scarcely conceivable that the tales could have remained so one-sided in their murders, rapes, seductions, fratricides, patricides, and plottings, had kingship in reality been a comfortable position of perquisites in a regular dynastic succession.

Nor was this merely a matter of open conflict over who should hold the throne. Behind that there emerged a more fundamental and, in the end, decisive issue. In promoting his own and his household's interests, the king-aristocrat became the agent of the community principle: the stronger the sense of community and the broader its powers, the greater the king and the more secure in his position. In reply the aristocracy demanded hegemony for the *oikos* and for their class, under a king if possible, without a king if need be. Homer records many incidents in this conflict and he makes no secret of his own preference for kingly rule, notably in his idealization of royal rule among the Phaeacians. He gives no clues to the outcome, but we know it well. By the time the *Odyssey* was written the de-

feat of the kings had been so complete that kingship was gone
from most of Hellas. In its place the aristocrats ruled as a
group, equals without a first among them.

And then the aristocrats found themselves with a new men-
ace, undreamed of in the world of Odysseus. The *demos,* nearly
always a passive bystander in the earlier political conflicts, began to know its own strength and capacity for rule. In the *Iliad*
and the *Odyssey* it grumbled or it acclaimed, but it took orders.
That was the recognized role of inferiors, to "honor him like
a god." On one occasion Agamemnon tried to use psychology
on his troops, with such ill success that panic set in and the
whole Greek army, become a mob, began to embark in disorder,
determined to sail for home and abandon the war. Hera intervened and sent Athena to Odysseus with instructions that he
pull himself together and put a stop to the disgraceful flight.
Taking Agamemnon's scepter, Odysseus went among the soldiers, cajoling and arguing as he moved.

"When he came to one who was a king and a man of emi-
nence, he stood beside him and restrained him with gentle
words. . . . But whatever man of the *demos* (i.e., commoner)
he saw and found him shouting, him he struck with the scepter,
upbraiding him in these words: 'Good sir, sit still and hearken
to the words of those who are your betters, you who are no
warrior and a weakling, who are not counted either in battle or
in council.' " [59]

That principle remained unchallenged in Odysseus' day.
Whatever the conflicts and cleavages among the noble households and families, they were always in accord that there
could be no crossing of the great line which separated the
aristoi from the many, the heroes from the non-heroes.

CHAPTER V

Morals and Values

Much of the twenty-third book of the *Iliad* is given over to an account of the funeral games staged by Achilles in honor of Patroclus. Before the assembled Achaean host the best athletes among the heroes competed in the traditional Greek contests: the chariot race and the foot race, boxing, wrestling, and weight-throwing, "and from his ships Achilles brought out prizes, caldrons and tripods and horses and mules and strong oxen, and also well-girdled women and gray iron." [1] The first event, described with fantastic power and brilliance, was the chariot race won by Diomedes. Nestor's son Antilochus barely defeated Menelaus for second place, but only because he had fouled the Spartan king on the far turn. Fourth came Meriones, and far to the rear poor Eumelus, thrown from his chariot when the yoke cracked, and forced to complete the course on foot, pulling the chariot behind him.

There was a prize for each competitor, in a sequence specified by Achilles beforehand. Diomedes immediately took the slave woman and tripod designated for the victor. Then Achilles proposed that Eumelus be given the second prize, a mare, as a mark of compassion for his sorry luck, and the audience as-

sented by acclamation, precisely as if they were sitting in formal
assembly Whereupon Antilochus "rose and spoke of his right.
'O Achilles, I shall be exceedingly angry with you if you carry
out what you have said.' " As for Eumelus, " 'he ought to have
prayed to the immortals, then he would not have come in last
of all in the race. If you have pity on him and he is dear to your
heart, you have much gold in your hut, you have copper and
sheep, you have slave women and uncloven horses. Take from
these and give him an even greater prize. . . . But this one I
will not give. For her, let him who will try battle at my hand.' "
Achilles smiled and conceded.

"But Menelaus also rose among them, sore at heart, full of
indignation at Antilochus. A herald placed the scepter in his
hand and bade the Argives be silent. And then the godlike
(*isotheos*, literally 'god-equal') man addressed them: 'Antilochus, you had been wise before, what kind of behavior was
this? You dishonored my valor and you interfered with my
horses, pushing ahead yours, which are very inferior. But come,
chieftains and leaders of the Argives, state the right between
the two of us.' "

Before the chieftains and leaders could state the right, however, Menelaus changed his mind and adopted an alternative
procedure. " 'Come now, I myself will state the right, and I believe that none of the Danaans will rebuke me, for it will be
straight. Antilochus, come here, fosterling of Zeus. According
to proper procedure (*themis*), stand before your horses and
chariot, take in your hand the thin whip with which you drove
before, and, with your hand on the horses, swear by (Poseidon)
the earth-mover and earth-shaker that you did not deliberately
interfere with my chariot by a trick.' " But Nestor's son, "who
had been wise" until his eagerness to win impelled him to

trickery, had recovered his wisdom by then, enough to refuse this challenge to perjure himself in the name of Poseidon. He apologized, offered the mare to Menelaus, and restored the peace.[2]

Homer gave this scene the outward form of a regular *agora,* which it unquestionably was not. Nor did it have to be. Menelaus demanded his right and he had the choice of methods, neither of which required an assembly. The issue between him and Antilochus could either be submitted to arbitration, as he first proposed, or it could be decided by oath. The two procedures were absolutely equal in validity and fully interchangeable; they were both ways of "stating the right," and they were both final, without appeal to any higher earthly authority. Should the answer turn out to be crooked, rather than straight, then the gods would have to arrange proper punishment. Had Antilochus, for example, accepted the challenge and perjured himself, beyond a doubt Poseidon would have taken merciless vengeance for so great an insult to his immortal name. But it was not the business of any mortal to raise the charge of false swearing.

The earlier issue of right was between Antilochus and Eumelus. Antilochus chose a third method, trial by armed combat. And the decision thus arrived at, had anyone taken him up, would also have been final: to the victor goes the right. There is a nice touch here, though an irrelevant one: between Antilochus and Eumelus there was no question of fact; Eumelus had finished last and Antilochus would have beaten him even if he had raced fairly. Nevertheless Antilochus could have chosen arbitration or the oath, just as Menelaus could have made trial with Antilochus by the sword. With variations in detail, these were the three ways, and the only three ways, that were available to the Homeric heroes for the settlement of disputes over rights.

Apart from the moment when the people acclaimed Achilles' gesture of compassion for Eumelus, the assemblage, heroes and *demos* alike, remained passive spectators. The defense of a right was a purely private matter. He who felt aggrieved had the responsibility to take the necessary steps and the right to choose from among the available methods. His kin or his guest-friends, retainers, and followers might intervene in support, but still as a private action. Although there are a few fragmentary phrases in the poems about royal judgments, they are contemporary notes, and therefore anachronistic, which slipped by the poet. He was composing at a time when the community principle had advanced to a point of some limited public administration of justice. But he was singing about a time when that was not the case, except for the intangible power of public opinion. How imposing a factor that was cannot be estimated, but it was surely significant and it must at times have led to intervention by outsiders to keep the peace. The principle remained, however, of strictly private rights privately protected. In no other way would the suitor theme of the *Odyssey* have been intelligible, and without the suitors' ruthless persistence and Telemachus's impotence there would have been no *Odyssey*.

Menelaus and Antilochus were equals in status. That was an essential fact, for justice among the heroes, like justice in the aristocratic code of honor of more modern times, was a matter for equals alone. Menelaus could no more have challenged Thersites to an oath than a Junker could have challenged a Berlin shopkeeper to a duel. Odysseus, we remember, stopped the panic in the Greek forces by appealing gently to the captains and by using the club and the command on the rank and file. The poet was not satisfied to close the scene on that note; instead he took the opportunity to write a little essay on social classes and the modes of behavior proper to each. Once Odysseus had succeeded in returning the men to the *agora,* the narrative took a new turn.

"Now all the others sat down and remained orderly in their seats; only Thersites the loose-tongued kept on scolding, he whose heart was full of words, many and disorderly, quarreling with the kings vainly and not in good order. . . . And he was the ugliest man who came to Ilion. He was bandy-legged and lame in one foot; his two shoulders were hunched and bent in upon his chest, and above them his head was misshapen, with sparse hair growing on it." The substance of Thersites' complaint was this: The devil with fighting to amass booty for Agamemnon; let us go home.

Odysseus strode to Thersites, ordered him to cease from his reviling of kings, and threatened to drive him naked and weeping from the assembly. "He spoke thus and beat him on the back and shoulders with the scepter. And he doubled up and a big tear fell from him, and a bloody welt rose on his back beneath the golden scepter. Then he sat down and was frightened; smarting with pain and looking foolish, he wiped away the tear. The others, though they were sorry, laughed lightly at him, and this is how one would speak, glancing at his neighbor: 'Oh yes! In truth Odysseus has done countless good things before, being pre-eminent in sound counsels and marshaling battles, but this is by far the best thing he has done among the Argives, that he has stopped this foul-mouthed slanderer from haranguing. Hardly, I think, will his arrogant heart again bid him rail at kings with words of reproach.' So spoke the multitude." ³

Those final words, "so spoke the multitude," protest too much. It is as if the poet himself felt that he had overdrawn the contrast. Do not think I talk from an aristocratic bias— that is the sense of the last four words. Even the commoners among the Hellenes stood aghast at Thersites' defective sense of fitness, and, though they pitied him as one of their own, they concurred with full heart in the rebuke administered by Odysseus and in the methods he employed. "This is by far the best thing he has done among the Argives" indeed, for Thersites had gnawed at the foundations on which the world of Odysseus was erected.

Of course Homer spoke for the aristocracy, from the opening line of the *Iliad* to the final sentence of the *Odyssey*. But what does that tell us? Does it mean, for example, that he is not to be trusted whenever he puts an idea or sentiment on the tongue of a Thersites or a Eumaeus? To answer that question in the affirmative would be to imagine a society in which aristocrats and commoners held two completely contradictory sets of values and beliefs, a society such as the world has never known. Beyond a doubt there were two standards in certain spheres of behavior, with respect to the ethos of work, for example, or in the protection of rights. Odysseus' employment of the scepter offers a fine symbol. On this occasion he had the use of Agamemnon's scepter, a gift from Zeus himself, fashioned by Hephaestus for the king of the gods, given by Zeus to Pelops, from whom it passed to Atreus, from Atreus to Thyestes, and then to Agamemnon, grandson of Pelops (it finally came to rest as a sacred relic in Plutarch's native city of Chaeronea).

The scepter, any scepter, was not only the symbol of authority; it was also the mark of *themis,* of orderly procedure, and so it was given to each assembly speaker in turn to secure his inviolability, as when Menelaus rose to challenge Antilochus. Against Thersites, however, it was a club, for Thersites was of those "who are not counted either in battle or in council." He harangued the assembly without *themis;* he had been given no scepter by the herald, therefore it was proper for him to receive it across the back.

The trouble is that we simply do not know how rights were determined when commoners were involved, whether between noble and commoner or between commoner and commoner. Neither Homer nor his audience cared about such matters, and we have no other source of information. This unconcern goes much deeper, extending to virtually the whole of the value scale. We are left to guess, and with little to base our guesses on. The evidence of what has been called the peasant type of heroic poetry, oral epics composed and recited among peasants rather than in the halls of barons—a very widespread type in many regions of Europe and Asia—tends to argue that they told the same kinds of stories, about the same kinds of heroes, with the identical values and virtues, as the aristocratic epic of the Homeric type. Against that there is the bitterness of Hesiod, with his peasant orientation, as well as the strong inference that in matters of religion, at least, Homer's indifference to the common people was actually a deliberate rejection of popular religious beliefs and practices. Presumably the commoner of Ithaca stood somewhere in the middle, sharing many notions and sentiments with Odysseus, but giving others a different coloring. By and large it is a useless exercise to seek these shadings. What we have on a very rich canvas are the morals and values of a warrior culture, and with that we must be content.

"Warrior" and "hero" are synonyms, and the main theme of a warrior culture is constructed on two notes—prowess and honor. The one is the hero's essential attribute, the other his essential aim. Every value, every judgment, every action, all skills and talents have the function of either defining honor or realizing it. Life itself may not stand in the way. The Homeric heroes loved life fiercely, as they did and felt everything with passion, and no less martyr-like characters could be imagined; but even life must surrender to honor. The two central figures of the *Iliad*, Achilles and Hector, were both fated to live short lives, and both knew it. They were heroes not because at the call of duty they marched proudly to their deaths, singing hymns to God and country—on the contrary, they railed openly against their doom, and Achilles, at least, did not complain less after he reached Hades—but because at the call of honor they obeyed the code of the hero without flinching and without questioning.

The heroic code was complete and unambiguous, so much so that neither the poet nor his characters ever had occasion to debate it. There were differences of opinion—whether to retreat in battle or not, whether to assassinate Telemachus or not, whether Odysseus was alive or dead—but these were either disagreements over matters of fact or tactical alternatives. In neither case was extended discussion called for. Or there were critical situations which demanded special knowledge, such as the plague that Apollo brought upon the Achaeans when they dishonored his priest. Then it was necessary to seek answer from the gods, and that fell to the soothsayer Calchas (among the Trojans there was Hector's brother Helenus, skilled in interpreting the flight of birds). Again there was no occasion for genuine discussion: the soothsayer gave the answer, and the heroes either obeyed or they did not, as their hearts bade them. Finally, there were moments when even the greatest of the heroes knew fear, but then it was enough to cry "Coward, woman!" to bring him back to his senses.

The significant fact is that never in either the *Iliad* or the *Odyssey* is there a rational discussion, a sustained, disciplined consideration of circumstances and their implications, of possible courses of action, their advantages and disadvantages. There are lengthy arguments, as between Achilles and Agamemnon, or between Telemachus and the suitors, but they are quarrels, not discussions, in which each side seeks to overpower the other by threats and to win over the assembled multitude by emotional appeal, by harangue, and by warning. Skill with words had its uses—Phoenix reminded Achilles that it was he who had taught him "to be both a speaker of words and a doer of deeds" [4]—in the struggle for public opinion. Never, however, was a dispute resolved by talk, but always by decision of the gods carried out through the prowess of the heroes.

The figure of Nestor is perhaps the most revealing in this regard. Eventually Nestor became the prototype of the wisdom of old age, the voice of experience, but Homer's Nestor was not that at all. Not once in his interminable talking did he draw upon his experience as the ground for choice between alternative procedures. In fact, throughout the *Iliad* he made but one suggestion that could in any proper sense be called a significant and reasoned one, his proposal that the Achaeans build a great defensive wall before their camp on the beach. With that single exception, Nestor's talk was invariably emotional and psychological, aimed at bolstering morale, not at steering the course of action. For that purpose his years of experience were very important, but in the unique sense of giving him the greatest store of incidents upon which to draw for models of heroic behavior, for reminders by example of the way to honor and glory. Odysseus, on the other hand, was the man of many devices, and his superior skill in that respect took the form of deception and mendacity. "Deceit and artful tales," Athena told him, not in criticism, are "dear to you from the bottom of your heart." [5] Odysseus lied all the time, on the assumption that it could do no harm and might turn out useful in the end; and he lied cleverly. This may have been purposeful deception in a general sense, but it was not controlled rational behavior. It was surely not wisdom.

The modern reader may be misled by the numerous formulas which, in one or another variant, speak of a man of counsel. For us counsel is deliberation; wise counsel, deliberation based on knowledge, experience, rational analysis, judgment. But counsel for Homer pointed less to the reasons than to the decision itself, and hence to the power of authority. Only in that sense could Nestor have called Agamemnon and Achilles "first of the Danaans both in counsel and in battle." [6] Neither was pre-eminent in the giving of advice—Achilles particularly not —but by status and power they outranked the others in the right of decision. There was much talk about a king's seeking counsel; and there was scarcely any offered that was more than encouragement or admonition. After all, the basic values of the society were given, predetermined, and so were a man's place in the society and the privileges and duties that followed from his status. They were not subject to analysis or debate, and other issues left only the narrowest margin for the exercise of what we should call judgment (as distinct from work skills, including knowledge of the tactics of armed combat).

There were situations in which one could legitimately disagree whether or not the counsel of prudence was also the voice of cowardice. Then it was not a question of mere tactics, nor the illegitimate one of challenging or defending the code of honor, but a matter of properly classifying and evaluating a specific choice of procedures. In the *Iliad* prudence was personified in the Trojan Polydamas (not in Nestor), and his interchanges with Hector underscored the true quality of the hero. Polydamas urged caution: Do not attack the Achaeans lest Achilles be roused and return to the fight and destroy us all. This was the prudent road to success, and Hector was utterly impatient with it, for it was not the road of honor. Polydamas was right, of course, and thanks to Hector's imprudent heroism the poem soon reached the final stage of preparation before the decisive single combat between Hector and Achilles. Prudence made one last attempt, this time in the persons of Priam and Hecuba, who begged their son not to fight Achilles, for the outcome was certain: Hector would be slain and Troy destroyed. Hector knew they were right in their prediction, as Polydamas had been earlier, and he said as much, but in a long soliloquy he rejected their plea and reasserted the paramount claim of honor. "I am ashamed before the Trojan men and the women of trailing robes, lest one worse than I should say: 'Hector by trusting in his own might has destroyed the people.' " What if I were to offer surrender and promise to return Helen and all her possessions and to pay in amends half the wealth of Troy? Achilles "would kill me, unarmed, as if but a woman." [7]

Rather than that Hector chose honorable death by combat, and the end of his city and his people. Once when Polydamas pointed to an ill omen as ground for caution, Hector brushed him off with "One omen is best, to fight back for one's fatherland." [8] But his whole course of behavior gave the lie to that retort. The fact is that such a notion of social obligation is fundamentally non-heroic. It reflects the new element, the community, at the one point at which it was permitted to override everything else, the point of defense against an invader. In the following generations, when the community began to move from the wings to the center of the Greek stage, the hero quickly died out, for the honor of the hero was purely individual, something he lived and fought for only for its sake and his own sake. (Family attachment was permissible, but that was because one's kin were indistinguishable from oneself.) The honor of a community was a totally different quality, requiring another order of skills and virtues; in fact, the community could grow only by taming the hero and blunting the free exercise of his prowess, and a domesticated hero was a contradiction in terms.

Achilles, a leader of the invading army, was not enmeshed in the extraneous strands of obligation. Writing long after Homer, Aeschylus could invent a scene in which the Myrmidons rebelled against Achilles for his refusal to fight. The Athenian playwright thus injected the notion of duty into the tale, but not once did Homer or Agamemnon or Odysseus charge Achilles with anything so anachronistic as public responsibility. Achilles was honor-bound to bring his incomparable prowess into the battle. But when Agamemnon took the girl Briseis from him his honor was openly shamed, and once "honor is destroyed the moral existence of the loser collapses." [9] The dilemma became at once unbearable: honor pulled in two opposing directions, and though one way pointed to victory in a great war and the other to a trifle, one captive woman out of thousands, the tremendous conflict lay precisely in the fact that honor was not measured like goods in a market, that the insult was worth as much as the war. Briseis was a trifle; but Briseis seized from Achilles was worth "seven tripods that have never been on the fire and ten talents of gold and twenty glittering caldrons" and twelve prize-winning racehorses and twenty Trojan captives and seven cities and a few other odds and ends.[10]

It was when Achilles refused this proper, and under all normal circumstances satisfactory, gift of amends that the real tragedy of the *Iliad* began. "Sing, goddess, of the wrath of Peleus' son Achilles." The hero's mistake was not made at the beginning; it came at the refusal of the penal gift, for that placed him temporarily beyond the heroic pale, that marked him as a man of unacceptable excesses. "Why," said Ajax in great indignation, "a man even accepts amends from the murderer of his brother or for his dead son, and the killer remains in his own country, having paid much. . . . But for you, the gods have put an implacable and evil emotion in your breast on account of a single girl." [11] Homer could not close the tale with the death of Hector at the hands of Achilles, for that would have left us with Achilles the too angry man, not with Achilles the redeemed hero. Achilles had still to expunge his wrath. This he did by abandoning his idea of throwing Hector's body to the dogs—a new excess, stemming from his grief over the death of Patroclus—and by returning the body to Priam for the proper rites. Now the slate was clean. Achilles had vindicated his honor on all sides, and had done so both honorably and with the fullest display of his prowess.

It is in the nature of honor that it must be exclusive, or at least hierarchic. When everyone attains equal honor, then there is no honor for anyone. Of necessity, therefore, the world of Odysseus was fiercely competitive, as each hero strove to outdo the others. And because the heroes were warriors, competition was fiercest where the highest honor was to be won, in individual combat on the field of battle. There a hero's ultimate worth, the meaning of his life, received its final test in three parts: whom he fought, how he fought, and how he fared. Hence, as Thorstein Veblen phrased it, under "this common-sense barbarian appreciation of worth or honor, the taking of life . . . is honorable in the highest degree. And this high office of slaughter, as an expression of the slayer's prepotence, casts a glamor of worth over every act of slaughter and over all the tools and accessories of the act." [12] The *Iliad* in particular is saturated in blood, a fact which cannot be hidden or argued away, twist the evidence as one may in a vain attempt to fit archaic Greek values to a more gentle code of ethics. The poet and his audience lingered lovingly over every act of slaughter: "Hippolochus darted away, and him too he (Agamemnon) smote to the ground; slicing off his hands with the sword and cutting off his neck, he sent him rolling like a round stone through the battle-throng." [13]

To Nietzsche the constant repetition of such scenes and their popularity throughout the Greek world for centuries to come demonstrated that "the Greeks, the most humane men of ancient times, have a trait of cruelty, a tigerish lust to annihilate." [14] But what must be stressed about Homeric cruelty is its heroic quality, not its specifically Greek character. In the final analysis, how can prepotence be determined except by repeated demonstrations of success? And the one indisputable measure of success is a trophy. While a battle is raging only the poet can observe Agamemnon's feat of converting Hippolochus into a rolling stone. The other heroes are too busy pursuing glory for themselves. But a trophy is lasting evidence, to be displayed at all appropriate occasions. Among more

primitive peoples the victim's head served that honorific purpose; in Homer's Greece armor replaced heads. That is why
time after time, even at great personal peril, the heroes paused
from their fighting in order to strip a slain opponent of his
armor. In terms of the battle itself such a procedure was not
merely absurd, it was almost treasonable, for it jeopardized the
fate of the whole expedition. It is a mistake in our judgment,
however, to see the battle as the goal, for victory without honor
was unacceptable; there could be no honor without public
proclamation, and there could be no publicity without the
evidence of a trophy.

In different ways this pattern of honor-contest-trophy reap-
peared in every activity. Achilles could find no more fitting
way to mourn his dead comrade than to set up a competitive
situation in which the Achaean nobles might display their
prowess. The moment Diomedes brought his chariot to the
finish line in first place he leaped to the ground and "he lost
no time; . . . eagerly he took the prize and gave his high-
spirited companions the woman to lead away and the tripod
with handles to carry; and he unyoked the horses." [15] This un-
selfconscious delight in the prizes, demonstrated before the ex-
cited assemblage, had little to do with their intrinsic worth;
Diomedes, like Achilles, had slave women and tripods enough
in his hut. His impetuosity—he did not even stop to attend to
his horses—was an emotional response, open and unabashed,
honor triumphant. We might call it a boyish gesture; for
Diomedes it was pride in his manliness.

The contest was to play a tremendous part in Greek public
life in later centuries. Nothing defines the quality of Greek culture more neatly than the way in which the idea of competition was extended from physical prowess to the realm of the

intellect, to feats of poetry and dramatic composition. For that step the world of Odysseus was of course unprepared. It was also unprepared to socialize the contest, so to speak. Diomedes sought victory in the chariot race, as on the battlefield, for himself alone, for the honor of his name and in a measure for the glory of his kin and companions. Later, when the community principle gained mastery, the *polis* shared in the glory, and in turn it arranged for victory songs and even public statues to commemorate the honor it, the city, had gained through one of its athletic sons. And with the replacement of the almost pure egoism of heroic honor by civic pride went still another change for which the Homeric world was unprepared: the laurel wreath took the place of gold and copper and captive women as the victor's prize.

Prestige symbols have a curious history. Among many primitive peoples they may be objects of little or no intrinsic worth, cowrie shells or wampum or cheap blankets. The world of Odysseus was not a primitive world, and in their higher sphere the Greeks of that time insisted on treasure. Their goal was honor, and the signs of honor are always conventional; but they would have nothing to do with conventional signs like cowrie. A beautiful young captive was a more honorific trophy than an old woman, and that was all there was to it. And then, in a still more advanced stage, the Greeks returned to cowrie shells— only they chose laurel wreaths instead. This Odysseus and his fellow nobles would simply not have understood. Even though the use of treasure was solely in display, solely in its prestige function, only its intrinsic worth gave it proper value.

Gift-giving too was part of the network of competitive, honorific activity. And in both directions: it was as honorable to give as to receive. One measure of a man's true worth was how much he could give away in treasure. Heroes boasted of the gifts they had received and of those they had given as signs of their prowess. That is why gift-objects had genealogies. When Telemachus refused Menelaus's offer of horses, the Spartan king countered with the following proposal: "Of the gifts, such as are treasures lying in my house, I will give you the one which is finest and most valuable. I will give you a skillfully wrought bowl; it is all of silver, finished with gold on the rim, the work of Hephaestus. The hero Phaedimus, king of the Sidonians, gave it to me." [16] A trophy with such a history obviously shed greater glory on both donor and recipient than just any silver bowl, as the armor of Hector was a far greater prize to his conqueror than the arms of one of the lesser Trojans. Status was the chief determinant of values, and status was transmitted from the person to his possessions, adding still more worth to their intrinsic value as gold or silver or fine woven cloth.

It was this honorific quality that distinguished the wealth of the heroes, and their almost overpowering accumulative instinct, from the materialistic drives of other classes and other ages. Wealth meant power and direct material satisfaction to Odysseus and his fellow nobles, to be sure, and that equation was never absent from their calculations. When Odysseus awakened on Ithaca, where the Phaeacians had landed him while he slept, he failed to recognize the island because Athena had covered it with a mist. His first reaction was one of anger that Alcinous and his men had broken faith and conducted him to some strange place. And almost in the same breath he began to worry about the gifts they had given him, lest they be stolen. Athena then appeared, quickly straightened him out, and personally helped him hide the treasure in a cave. Later, in his first meeting with Penelope, Odysseus in disguise deliberately

misled her with an elaborate tale which ended with the story
that he had but recently met the long-lost hero in Thesprotia,
from which country "he is bringing much good treasure as he
begs up and down the land." He would have returned sooner,
"but it seemed to his heart more advantageous to collect much
goods as he went over the earth." [17]

The tale was false, but as the poet said, it was "in the like-
ness of truth." [18] Odysseus actually used the word "to beg"
(*aitizo*), the very word Eumaeus had used when he advised his
disguised master to go into town and beg for food. But what
Odysseus meant and what Eumaeus meant were altogether different. A king "begged" for gifts of treasure as part of the normal course of his travels and his relations abroad, with kin
and guest-friends, old and new, as a way of adding new links
to the endless chain of gift and counter-gift. When King Alcinous asked him to remain overnight so that the proper parting gifts could be assembled, Odysseus replied: I would wait
a year if necessary, "for more advantageous would it be to come
to my dear fatherland with a fuller hand, and so should I be
more reverenced and loved among men, whosoever should see
me after I returned to Ithaca." [19] This he said in the same court
in which he had reacted so violently to the suggestion that he
might be a trader seeking "greedy gains."

There were delicate distinctions here, between honorable acquisition and greedy gain. The heroes had a streak of the peasant
in them, and with it went a peasant's love of possessions, a cal-
culating, almost niggardly hoarding and measuring and count-
ing. But the heroes were more than peasants, and they could
give as proudly as they took, and they could set honor above
all material goods. The same Achilles who reminded Agamemnon that "it was not on account of the Trojan warriors that

I came here to fight, for they have committed no offense against me: they have not robbed me of my cattle or my horses," [20] could reject with utter contempt Agamemnon's compensatory gifts, fabulous as they were: "For cattle and fine sheep can be rustled, and tripods and chestnut horses can be acquired." [21] The circulation of treasure was as essential a part of heroic life as its acquisition; and it was this movement, the fact of its existence and the orbits it followed, that set that life apart from any other life of accumulation.

What tends to confuse us is the fact that the heroic world was unable to visualize any achievement or relationship except in concrete terms. The gods were anthropomorphized, the emotions and feelings were located in specific organs of the body, the soul was materialized. Every quality or state had to be translated into some specific symbol, honor into a trophy, friendship into treasure, marriage into gifts of cattle. In the furious quarrel with Agamemnon, Achilles reached such a point of wrath that he drew his sword. Athena promptly appeared beside him, unseen to anyone else, and checked him with a command curiously put in the language of a plea, and ending with these words: "For thus do I declare, and it shall come to pass: hereafter shall splendid gifts come to you in threefold measure, because of this (Agamemnon's) insolence; but restrain yourself and hearken to us." [22] This was the only intelligible language of pleading, and by gifts the goddess meant material goods, not blessings of the spirit.

Because the concrete expressions of honor and friendship were always articles of explicit value, not cowrie shells, the prestige element was concealed under an overlay of treasure. In fact, both counted greatly, the wealth as wealth on the one hand, and the wealth as symbol on the other. That is why the giving and receiving were ceremonial acts, an added touch that would have been utterly needless were possession sufficient unto itself. King Alcinous personally stowed the Phaeacian gifts aboard Odysseus' ship, as the head of a modern state personally signs a treaty before assembled dignitaries. In a significant sense the gifts of guest-friendship were the archaic forerunners of articles of agreement. What other firm proof could there have been, in that unlettered world, that a relationship had been established, creating obligations and responsibilities?

At no point was the bond between ceremonialism and the satisfaction of material wants more tightly knit than in the endless feasting. "For I say that there is nothing more gracious than when one has good cheer among the whole population, and the sharers in the feast in all the homes, seated in order, listen to the minstrel, and the tables alongside them are laden with bread and meat, and the cupbearer draws wine from the mixing-bowl and serves it around and pours it into the goblets." [23] Odysseus was weary. After ten years of war and another ten years of the most incredible and taxing adventures he had come to the Phaeacian Utopia, and his mind was reaching out to his own home, to the approaching end of his wanderings. He began to relax, and he made this pretty little speech.

But there was more than good cheer and *Gemütlichkeit* to Homeric feasting. "Idomeneus," said Agamemnon, "I honor you above all the Danaans of the fleet horses, whether in war or in some other work or in the feast, when the Argive nobles mix the sparkling wine of the elders in the bowl." [24] This formulation of the hierarchy of aristocratic activities, setting the banquet alongside the battle and "other work," was precise, for it was feasting that occupied the heroes when they were not immediately engaged in the pursuits of combat, and it was heroic feasting, not only in its magnitude but also in its ethics. What was blameworthy about the suitors, for example, was not the total idleness and luxury of their daily banqueting in the halls of Odysseus. That was proper aristocratic behavior, but it was most improper to carry on the feasting at one man's expense, all the more so when it was done in his absence. "Sharers in the feast" was the phrase (one word in the Greek) Odysseus used in Phaeacia, and by it he meant those who shared the cost as well as the pleasures. "Leave my palace," Telemachus demanded of the suitors in all earnestness, with no trace of mockery, "and hold your feasts elsewhere, eating your own substance, going from house to house in turn." [25]

Just as there could be no ceremonial occasion without gifts of treasure, so there could be none without a feast. The *Iliad* closes with the Trojan mourning for Hector. For nine days they mourned, and on the tenth they cremated his body, placed the bones in a golden urn, and buried them in the presence of the assembled Trojan army. "And having heaped the burial mound, they went back; then they gathered together and feasted well in a glorious feast in the house of Priam, the king nourished by Zeus. Thus they performed the funeral rites for Hector, tamer of horses." [26] Or, to take a different example, there is Nestor's advice to Agamemnon: "Give a feast for the elders, that is proper for you and not unseemly." [27] On such occasions, of course, there was no sharing of cost; Priam gave the feast that closed the funeral rites, and Agamemnon feasted his council of elders before they deliberated.

The meaning of this ceremonial eating together becomes clearest in still another context. Without exception, whenever a visitor arrived, whether kin or guest-friend, emissary or stranger, the first order of business was the sharing of a meal.

This was a rule on all levels, when Odysseus, Ajax, and Phoenix came to Achilles with Agamemnon's proposal of a gift of amends, or when the then unidentified beggar appeared at the hut of Eumaeus the slave and swineherd. Only after the meal was it proper for the host to inquire who his guest was and what his mission. "But come along," said Eumaeus, "let us go into the hut, old man, so that after you have satisfied yourself with bread and wine to your heart's content, you may tell whence you are and how many troubles you have suffered." [28]

This was a ritual that could not be refused, akin to the taboo-purging rituals of the primitive world. Hence the meal was shared not merely by host and guest and their retainers, but also by the gods. "Then the swineherd stood up and carved . . . and he divided and distributed the whole into seven portions. The first he set aside for the nymphs and for Hermes son of Maia, having prayed, and the others he distributed to each . . . and he made burnt offering to the everlasting gods." [29] The descriptions of the sacrifices vary, and so do the names of the participating gods, but the essential notion was always the same. Through the sharing of food—in substantial quantities, it should be noted, not just symbolically—a bond was instituted, or renewed, in ceremonial fashion, tying men and gods, the living and the dead, into an ordered universe of existence. It was as if the constant repetition of the feast were somehow necessary for the preservation of the group, whether on the *oikos* level or on the larger scale of the class, and also for the establishment of peaceful relations across lines, with strangers and guest-friends.

Conversely, exclusion from the feast was the mark of the social outcast. Upon learning of the death of Hector, Andromache in her great grief lamented the fate in store for the boy

Astyanax: "And in his need the child turns to his father's companions, pulling one by the cloak, another by the tunic; and of those who take pity one gives him a sip, and he moistens his lips, but his palate he does not moisten. And some unorphaned child drives him from the feast with blows of the hand, reviling him with abuse: 'Away, you! Your father does not share the feast with us.' " [30]

Andromache could not protect her child, not even in her imagination, for women had no place at the feast. Not only was this a man's world, it was one in which the inferior status of women was neither concealed nor idealized, which knew neither chivalry nor romantic attachments. "Do they then alone of mortal men love their wives, these sons of Atreus?" Achilles is quoted as asking, according to the usual translations.[31] The Greek, however, does not say "wives," it says "bed-mates"; Achilles was speaking of a woman he had "won with the spear." Earlier Agamemnon had said of Chryseis, the priest's captive daughter, "Yes, I prefer her to Clytaemnestra, my wedded bed-mate." [32] In fact, from Homer to the end of Greek literature there were no ordinary words with the specific meanings "husband" and "wife." A man was a man, a father, a warrior, a nobleman, a chieftain, a king, a hero; linguistically he was almost never a husband.

And then there is the word "to love." That is how we render *philein,* but the question remains open as to what emotional quality, what overtones, the Greek verb really possessed. It was used in every context in which there were positive ties between people. When he visited Aeolus, keeper of the winds, Odysseus reported, "he treated me hospitably for a full month," [33] and *philein* was the word by which hospitable treatment was expressed. But where in the many references to Odysseus' sad longing for his home and his wife is there a passage in which sentiments and passions that the modern world calls "love" shine through? More often than not Penelope was omitted from the image of home, for the standard formula was the one used by Nausicaa: "Then there is hope that you will see your friends, and come to your home good to dwell in, and to your native land." [34]

Odysseus was fond of Penelope, beyond a doubt, and he found her sexually desirable. She was part of what he meant by "home," the mother of his dear son and the mistress of his *oikos*. Monogamous marriage was the absolute rule: there are no confirmed bachelors in the poems, and no spinsters, and the sole reference to divorce is the somewhat dubious one in which Hephaestus threatened to return his adulterous wife, Aphrodite, to her father (a threat that was not carried out).[35] The meaning of monogamy must not be misconstrued, however. It neither imposed monogamous sexuality on the male nor did it place the small family at the center of a man's emotional life. The language had no word at all for the small family, in the sense in which one might say, "I want to go back to live with my family."

Neither in the relationship between Odysseus and Penelope nor in any other relationship between man and mate in the Homeric poems was there the depth and intensity, the quality of feeling—on the part of the male—that marked the attachment between father and son on the one hand, and between male and male companion on the other. The poems are rich in such images as this: "as a father greets his dear son who has come from a distant land in the tenth year"; [36] but there are no similes drawn from a husband's joy in his wife. In the narrative itself one need only recall the key role of the love of Achilles for

Patroclus, and the massive grief of Achilles at the death of his comrade.

There is an ancient dispute, still unresolved, whether overt eroticism was part of the relationship between Achilles and Patroclus. The text of the poems offers no directly affirmative evidence at any point; even the two references to the elevation of Ganymede to Olympus speak only of his becoming cup-bearer to Zeus. Pederasty was a widely accepted practice in the Greek world at a very early date, and it remained an integral part of Greek culture for many centuries, as the literature from Theognis to Plato eloquently testifies. What was involved, furthermore, was not homosexuality in the sense of the direction of erotic impulses and activity exclusively to members of one's own sex, but a full bisexuality. Neither Greek practice nor Greek ethics, therefore, would have seen anything inconsistent or unlikely in the coexistence of an erotic relationship between heroes and their vaunted prowess with the opposite sex. If historical proof is needed, it is enough to point to the warrior elites of Sparta and Thebes. And so, to explain the striking intensity of Achilles' passion and to fit the world of Odysseus into the mainstream of Hellenic culture, it has been argued that on this matter we are faced with another instance of "expurgation" in the poems, that "Homer has swept this whole business, root and branch, out of his conception of life." [37]

Be that as it may, there is no mistaking the fact that Homer fully reveals what remained true for the whole of antiquity, that women were held to be naturally inferior and therefore limited in their function to the production of offspring and the performance of household duties, and that the meaningful social relationships and the strong personal attachments were sought and found among men. The classic exposition may be read in the eighth book of Aristotle's *Nicomachean Ethics*, on *philia*, which we render with the pale word "friendship." When there is *philia* of a lower kind, says Aristotle, between unequal partners, as between a man and a woman, "each of the two differs in virtue and function, in the ground for friendship, and therefore also in affection and friendship." Accordingly, the affection should be proportionate to the respective worths of each: "the better (of the two), for example, should receive more affection than he gives." [38] And that is precisely what we find in Homer. While Odysseus was absent the loss to Penelope, emotionally, psychologically, affectively, was incomparably greater than the loss to her husband. The grief of Achilles was nearly matched by the sorrow of Hecuba and Andromache at the death of Hector, son to one and husband to the other.

Some caution must be exercised here. What we have is a skillfully shaped portrayal of the second sex, in which a bard who fully shared the conviction of the natural inferiority of women defined their feelings to their lords and superiors. The image which emerges is a complicated one, and in some respects an enigmatic one. The two characters in the poems who are not fully resolved are both women, Arete, queen of the Phaeacians, with her strange, unwomanly claims to power and authority, and Helen, who is a very peculiar figure. Helen, daughter of Zeus and Leda, was Aphrodite's favorite, and thanks to the gifts of the goddess she succeeded in embroiling Greeks and Trojans in a gigantic struggle that cost both sides dearly. Helen was no innocent victim in all this, no unwilling captive of Paris-Alexander, but an adulteress in the most complete sense. For Paris there was no atonement. "Lord Zeus," prayed Menelaus, "grant that I be avenged on him who first did me wrong, illustrious Alexander, and subdue him at my hands, so that any man born hereafter may shrink from wronging a host who has shown him friendship." [39] But Helen received no punishment, and scarcely any reproach. She ended her days back in Sparta, administering magical drugs obtained in Egypt, interpreting omens, and participating in the life of the palace much like Arete and not like a proper Greek woman.

Not even Penelope was altogether free of suspicion and the element of enigma. When Athena bade Telemachus return immediately from his visit to Menelaus, lest Penelope, who was weakening under pressure from her father and brothers, not only accept one of the suitors but strip the palace of treasure to boot, the goddess concluded with a sweeping generalization: "For you know what is the emotion in the breast of a woman, that she wishes to increase the household of him who weds her, and of her former children and of her dear husband she neither remembers once he is dead nor inquires." [40]

This was a strange way indeed to talk about Penelope, and it came from a very interesting source. On Olympus the gods were altogether superior to the goddesses, considered collectively—superior not only in their power but also in their appeal, in the feelings they inspired among men. The chief exception to the rule was Athena, and the significant quality of Athena as a goddess was her manliness. She was the virgin goddess in a world that knew no original sin, no sinfulness of sex, no Vestal Virgins. She was not even born of woman, having sprung from the head of Zeus—an insult to the whole race of women for which Hera never forgave her husband, Hera who was the complete female and whom the Greeks feared a little and did not like at all, from the days of Odysseus to the twilight of the gods.

Neither Athena nor the poet went further in explaining

Penelope's behavior. The responsibility for Helen, however, was explicitly Aphrodite's. Early in the *Iliad*, Paris engaged Menelaus in single combat and was within an inch of losing his life when "Aphrodite snatched him up most easily, being a god, and covered him with a heavy mist and set him down in his fragrant, incense-smelling chamber. And she herself went to summon Helen" from the battlements. " 'Come here. Alexander summons you to go home. He is there in his chamber and inlaid bed.' " Helen demurred. "Then angrily divine Aphrodite addressed her: 'Do not provoke me, wretch, lest in my wrath I abandon you, and in this wise hate you as now I love you beyond measure.' " [41] And Helen was afraid, and she took herself to the fragant chamber and the inlaid bed.

The reason for Helen's reluctance had been given some verses before. In the guise of Laodice, Priam's fairest daughter, the divine messenger Iris had talked with her and had "placed in her heart sweet yearning for her former husband and her city and parents." [42] This impasse in which Helen was placed was nothing unusual, for in the Homeric psychology every human action and every idea, especially if it departed in any way from the normal or the expected, was the direct consequence of divine interposition. When Eurycleia informed Penelope that Odysseus had returned and destroyed the suitors, the queen replied in utter disbelief: "Good mother, the gods have made you mad, they who are able to make witless even those with the best wit, and they bring the weak-minded to prudence. They have distracted you, who were formerly right-minded." [43] The examples can be multiplied from every page and in every conceivable situation. So far-reaching was this conception of the nature of man that Homer has no word for an act of deliberate choice or decision.

Nowhere is the historian faced with a more subtle problem. Was all this literal belief or poetic metaphor? When the heroes are called *dios* (divine), *isotheos* (god-equal), *diotrephes* (nourished by Zeus), precisely what significance shall we attach to the epithets? * What did they mean to the poet and his audience? When Menelaus began to drag Paris in the dust and Aphrodite tore off the latter's helmet-strap just before it strangled him, was that a fancy poetic figure for chance, for a lucky accident that broke the strap in time, or did Homer believe literally what he sang? Above all, what of the genealogies, which gave every aristocratic family, and even whole tribes, divine ancestry? Poseidon was angered beyond measure by the Phaeacians because they not only rescued Odysseus but returned him to Ithaca laden with treasure, and his anger was compounded by the fact that the Phaeacians "come from my own stock." 44 In Odysseus' account of his journey to Hades there is one lengthy section which serves no purpose other than to parade various women proud to have born mortal sons to Zeus or Poseidon. The converse was exceedingly rare—Calypso even protested: "You are merciless, you gods, and jealous beyond compare, who begrudge goddesses that they have intercourse with men openly, if one makes one her dear bedfellow." 45 From one such union came Achilles, son of Peleus and of Thetis the sea-nymph; from another, Aeneas, son of Anchises and Aphrodite.

It is inconceivable that this passion for divine genealogy was mere poetic fancy. Here was sanction for aristocratic privilege, for rule by might, and an ideology that no one believes is an absurdity. Xenophanes, in the sixth century, was not tilting at windmills when he raised his voice in the sharpest possible pro-

* Following an accepted convention, I have translated *dios* as "illustrious" throughout.

test against the Homeric view of the gods. If "theft, adultery, and deceit" were commonly accepted as divine practices, then surely divine ancestry of mortals and divine intervention in battle were scarcely less credible. The irrelevance of so many of the interventions, which contribute nothing to the development of the narrative, is a further argument. Undoubtedly there is much here that was part of the inherited bardic formulas, repeated and perpetuated after much of primitive belief had degenerated into mere clichés of speech and story-telling. The essential difficulty is to find the proper line between a primitive thought-world that was gone and a rationality that was yet to come.

One element which was decidedly not primitive was the complete anthropomorphism. God was created in man's image with a skill and a genius that must be ranked with man's greatest intellectual feats. The whole of heroic society was reproduced on Olympus in its complexities and its shadings. The world of the gods was a social world in every respect, with a past and a present, with a history, so to speak. There was no Genesis, no creation out of nothing. The gods came to power on Olympus as men came to power in Ithaca or Sparta or Troy, through struggle and family inheritance. Here is the account in Poseidon's words of what followed the forcible overthrow of the Titans: "For we are three brothers, sons of Cronus, whom Rhea bore, Zeus and I, and Hades is the third, who rules the underworld. And in three lots we divided everything, and each drew his share of honor (i.e., his domain): I drew the white sea to inhabit forever, when we cast lots, and Hades drew the murky darkness, and Zeus drew the wide heaven, in air and clouds; but the earth and high Olympus are common to all." [46]

These sentences were part of a very angry speech. Poseidon

had entered the battle on the Greek side, and the Trojans were in rout. Zeus sent Iris to him with an order that he withdraw from the fight. "Highly indignant, the renowned earth-shaker answered her: 'Oh no, for strong as he is, he has spoken insolently if he will master me by force, against my will, I who am his equal in honor.' " [47] Poseidon gave in, of course, but in the colloquy the parallel between gods and heroes was perfectly drawn. Like any hero, Poseidon was concerned solely with honor and prowess. He bowed to the authority of Zeus, but only because the elder brother was prepotent. Earlier, when Hera first proposed that together they could outmaneuver Zeus and save the Achaeans from the slaughter that was planned for them, Poseidon would have none of it. "Hera reckless in speech, what manner of talk have you spoken! I would not see us all at war with Zeus Cronion, for he is far greater." [48]

With respect to power, the divine world was as differentiated as the human, and the range was very wide. Not only were there great differences in the quantity possessed by the individual gods, there were also significant distinctions in the spheres in which power could be applied. Aphrodite, for example, was invincible in matters of erotic desire. But when she tried to take part in the actual fighting, Diomedes attacked her, "knowing that she was a feeble god," [49] and he wounded her in the hand. Aphrodite went weeping to Zeus, only to receive a gentle rebuke: "Not to you, my child, are given the works of war, but do you pursue the loving works of wedlock and all these will be looked to by fleet Ares and Athena." [50]

Only Zeus occupied a position without earthly parallel. His power was too overwhelming, such as not even the greatest king could dream of. And Zeus maintained a distance between himself and the mortal world that was also unique. He alone of the Olympians never intervened directly in speech or act, but through a verbal message carried by Iris, Dream, Rumor, or one of the other gods, or through the still less direct form of an omen, such as thunder or the flight of an eagle. Even on Olympus there was distance: when Zeus entered his palace, "all the gods rose at once from their seats in the presence of their father." [51] It would be a mistake, however, to imagine Zeus as some kind of Eastern potentate. For all his uniqueness, he had much of the Greek *basileus* in him (though Homer never gave him the title), a special sort of first among equals. The *Odyssey* opens with an appeal by Athena that he put an end to the travail of Odysseus. In reply Zeus first denied responsibility for what was happening. "It is Poseidon the earth-mover who has stubbornly remained angry, because of the Cyclops whom he (Odysseus) blinded in the eye." Then Zeus proposed a course of action: "But come, let us all here consider his homecoming, that he might return. Poseidon will give up his anger, for he will be powerless against all the immortals, striving alone against the will of the gods." [52]

This mixture of might and counsel bespoke the archaic world. Even Poseidon admitted the power of Zeus to compel obedience, and yet the poet was reluctant to reduce the decision to force alone. He was not always able to achieve full consistency in the heavenly picture: the case of Zeus is outstanding, but there are others, such as the two conceptions of fate, one that it was the work of the gods and the other that it bound all, mortals and immortals alike; or the notion of Hades as neutral, as a place where the shades of men live on in utter dullness and emptiness, but where, nevertheless, a few like Tantalus are doomed to everlasting torment. The inconsistencies merely point up how tremendous was the effort to recreate the heroic world on another plane, and how very successful it was. The evidence can be drawn from every sphere, from wealth and labor, gift-giving and feasting, honor and shame.

A measure of failure was inevitable. That the gods were immortal was one source of difficulty, but perhaps not the chief one. Because they could not die, the gods could not be true heroes. They might fail to attain a specific goal, but there was never any risk in the attempt. Still, it was possible to overlook that one flaw and to have the gods behave otherwise exactly as heroes would behave. It was possible, too, to take care of minor technicalities of immortality: blood was the physiological key to mortality, and therefore it had to be replaced by another substance, called ichor. What was not possible was to define power in purely human terms, even on the most heroic scale. Divine power was supernatural in the precise sense. It was superior to human power in its quality, in its magic. Diomedes could defeat Aphrodite in direct combat, but only so long as the feeble goddess failed to avail herself of the supernatural powers that even she commanded. She could have covered him with a heavy mist and snatched him up and away, for instance. Against such arts Achilles himself would have been outmatched. Only the gods, further, had the power to take a man's wits from him, or to teach bards and seers to know things that had been and things that were to be.

The humanization of the gods was a step of astonishing boldness. To picture supernatural beings not as vague, formless spirits, or as monstrous shapes, half bird, half animal, for instance, but as men and women, with human organs and human passions, demanded the greatest audacity and pride in one's own humanity. Then, having so created his gods, Homeric man called himself godlike. The words "man" and "godlike" must be stressed sharply. On the one hand, Homer never confused "godlike" with "divine"; he never crossed the line between the mortal and the immortal. Hesiod spoke of "a godlike race of hero-men who are called demi-gods," but there were no demi-gods in the *Iliad* or *Odyssey*. Kings were honored like gods, but never worshiped. Heroes were men, not cult objects. Though they had divine ancestors, blood ran in their veins nonetheless, not ichor. On the other hand, there were no local, regional, or national dividing lines of genuine consequence among men. Neither in matters of cult nor in any other fundamental aspect of human life did the poet distinguish or classify invidiously. Individuals and classes varied in worth and capacity, but not peoples, neither between Achaeans and others nor among the Achaeans themselves. This universality of Homer's humanity was as bold and remarkable as the humanity of his gods.

That we are faced here with a new creation, a revolution in religion, can scarcely be doubted. We do not know who accomplished it, whether the poet of the *Iliad* or some earlier bard, but we can be sure that a sudden transformation occurred, not just a slow, gradual shift in beliefs. Never in the history of the known religions, Eastern or Western, was a new religion introduced otherwise than at one stroke. New ideas may have been germinating for a long time, old ideas may have been undergoing constant and slow change, still other notions may have been imported from abroad. But the actual step of transformation, the abandonment of the old faith and the creation of the new, has always been sharp, swift, abrupt.

Traces of the shift are still visible in the Homeric poems. The old nature gods survived, for instance, but they were debased or ignored. Helius, the sun, was so impotent that when Odys-

seus' starving men committed the terrible offense of killing
some of his cattle he could do no better than rush to Zeus and
ask the latter to take vengeance for him. Selene, the moon, was
of no consequence whatsoever. Most notable of all is the indifference to Demeter, goddess of fertility, for, unlike Helius and
Selene, Demeter remained a major figure in Greek religion for
many centuries after Homer. Her rites celebrated the procession of the seasons, the mystery of the plants and the fruits in
their annual cycle of coming to be and passing away. Demeter-
worship was carried on outside the formal Olympian religion,
for its founder had place neither for her nor for mystery rites
altogether.

Homer knew all about Demeter (she is mentioned six times
in the *Iliad* and *Odyssey*); and that is just the point. He deliberately turned his back on her and everything she represented. "Honor him like a god with gifts" is a recurrent phrase
about kings; the converse is that the gods are to be honored
like kings with gifts. In practice that meant gifts of food, of
feasting, through burnt offerings, and gifts of treasure, through
dedications of arms and caldrons and tripods arrayed in the
temples. The temples and their priests, incidentally, were themselves part of the new religion. The forces of nature had been
worshiped where they were; the gods conceived as men were
housed, like men, in appropriate palaces. Mystery rites (literally
"orgies," a word which does not appear in either poem) and
blood rites and human sacrifice and everything else that de-
humanized the gods were ruthlessly discarded. Thus the important story of the sacrifice of Agamemnon's daughter Iphigenia was omitted, and the many gross atrocities in the prehistory of the gods were toned down radically. Achilles, it is

true, sacrificed "twelve brave sons of great-hearted Trojans" on the funeral pyre of Patroclus, but the poet promptly labeled that act of primitive horror for what it was: "such evil deeds did he contrive in his heart." [53]

In a famous passage in his autobiography, John Stuart Mill wrote of his father: "I have a hundred times heard him say that all ages and nations have represented their gods as wicked, in a constantly increasing progression; that mankind have gone on adding trait after trait till they reached the most perfect conception of wickedness which the human mind can devise, and have called this God, and prostrated themselves before it." For Homeric religion, at least, this is not a pertinent judgment, not because Homer's gods were not wicked, but because they were essentially devoid of any ethical quality whatsoever. The ethics of the world of Odysseus were man-made and man-sanctioned. Man turned to the gods for help in his manifold activities, for the gifts it was in their power to offer or to withhold. He could not turn to them for moral guidance; that was not in their power.

When Odysseus awoke on Ithaca, Athena appeared to him in the guise of a shepherd and was greeted by one of Odysseus' characteristic inventions, how he came from Crete, fought at Troy, slew the son of Idomeneus, fled to the Phoenicians, and so forth. Athena smiled, resumed her female shape, and offered the following comment: "Crafty must he be and shifty who would outstrip you in all kinds of cunning, even though it be a god that encountered you. Headstrong man, full of wiles, of cunning insatiate, are you not to cease, even in your own land, from deceit and artful tales, so dear to you from the bottom of your heart? But come, let us speak no more of these things, being both practiced in craft; for you are far the best of all mortals in counsel and speech, and I am celebrated among all the gods in craft and cunning." [54]

This is what the long line of philosophers from Xenophanes to Plato protested, the indifference of the Homeric gods in moral matters. Just before the close of the *Iliad,* Achilles stated the doctrine explicitly: "For two jars stand on Zeus's threshold whence he gives of his evil gifts, and another of the good; and to whom Zeus who delights in thunder gives a mixed portion, to him befalls now evil, now good; but to whom he gives of the baneful, him he scorns, and evil misery chases him over the noble earth, a wanderer honored neither by gods nor by mortals." [55]

Chance, not merit, determined how the gifts fell to a man. And since it was not in his power to influence the choice, man could neither sin nor atone. He could offend a god mightily, but only by dishonoring him, by shaming him—through a false oath, for example, or disobedience of the direct command of an oracle or failure to make a sacrificial gift—and then it was incumbent upon the offender to make amends precisely as he made amends to any man he might have dishonored. But this was not penance; it was the re-establishment of the proper status relationship. Without sin there could be no idea of conscience, no feelings of moral guilt. The evils of which Achilles spoke were mishaps, not the evils of the Decalogue.

And there was no reverential fear of the gods. "Homer's princes bestride their world boldly; they fear the gods only as they fear their human overlords." [56] No word for "god-fearing" is ever used in the *Iliad.* Nor, it scarcely need be added, was there a word for "love of God": *philotheos* makes its first appearance in the language with Aristotle. For moral support the men of the *Iliad* relied not on the gods but on their fellow men, on the institutions and the customs by which they lived; so complete was the intellectual revolution that had occurred. Having lifted the incubus of unintelligible and all-powerful natural forces, man retained a consciousness that there were powers in the universe which he could not control and could not really understand, but he introduced a great self-consciousness, a pride and a confidence in himself, in man and his ways in society.

But what of the men whose life gave no warrant for pride and self-confidence? For it is self-evident that the gods of the *Iliad* were the gods of heroes, or, plainly spoken, of the princes and the heads of the great households. What of the others, those for whom the iron age had come, when "men never rest from labor and sorrow by day, and from perishing by night"? [57] They had reason enough to fear the gods, but they had no reason to be god-fearing if the gods were truly as the poet described them. For them there was little question of choice of gifts; there was always the certainty that the gifts would come from the wrong jar: "Evil misery chases him over the noble earth, a wanderer honored neither by gods nor by mortals." The poet of the *Iliad* could turn away from Demeter in contempt, but to the iron race of men she gave promise of a harvest, as the god Dionysus, whom Homer also ignored, meant wine and joy and forgetfulness of sorrow. "Apollo moved only in the best society, from the days when he was Hector's patron to the days when he canonized aristocratic athletes; but Dionysus was at all periods *demotikos*, a god of the people." [58]

The Olympian religion could not stand still and yet survive. The intellectual revolution reflected in the *Iliad* required still another revolution, a moral one, in which Zeus was transformed

from the king of a heroic society to the principle of cosmic justice. There are elements of this new conception in the *Odyssey*,
for the suitor theme is in some fashion a tale of villainy and retribution. "Father Zeus," said old Laertes when Odysseus revealed himself and told him of the slaughter of the suitors,
"indeed you gods still exist on high Olympus, if truly the wooers
have paid for their evil insolence." [59] The contrast with the
Iliad is striking. There the destruction of Troy was, if anything,
an act of divine injustice. Paris had insulted Menelaus, and
both sides, Achaeans and Trojans alike, were prepared at one
point to rest the decision on single combat between the two
heroes. Menelaus was the victor, and the war should have
ended then, with the return of Helen and the payment of
amends, but Hera and Athena would not be content until Ilion
was sacked and all its men killed. The interest of the two goddesses was strictly heroic, an insistence on full retribution for
the shame they once had suffered at the hands of Paris when
he judged Aphrodite more beautiful. This and nothing else
brought about the fall of Troy.

Zeus bowed to Hera's demand, even though, in his own
words, "of all the cities under the sun and the starry heaven in
which dwell earthly men, most honored of my heart was holy
Ilion, and Priam and the people of Priam of the good ashen
spear." Hera responded in kind: "Indeed there are three cities
most dear of all to me, Argos and Sparta and wide-wayed
Mycenae. These lay waste whenever they become hateful to
your heart; for them I shall neither stand up nor hold a
grudge." [60] For the decision to be put into effect, it should be
added, Athena was called upon to trap the Trojans, by the
most malicious deception, into violating the oaths they and the

Achaeans had taken when Menelaus and Paris met in single combat.

From such a view of divine motives to the punishment of the suitors was a long step, and the poet of the *Odyssey* took it hesitantly and incompletely. Its implications were extensive and complex, and he did not always see them by any means. When he did, the effect was startling. No sooner had Eurycleia returned to the great chamber of the palace and seen the carnage among the suitors, then "she was about to cry out in exultation, beholding so great a deed. But Odysseus restrained her. . . . 'Rejoice in your heart, old woman, and restrain yourself and do not cry aloud. It is an unholy thing to glory over slain men. These men the destiny of the gods has overpowered, and their (own) merciless deeds.' " [61] Not only was this sentiment unheroic, for heroes commonly exercised their prerogative to exult publicly over their victims, but in a sense it remained un-Hellenic, as Nietzsche's dictum suggests. It was as if, groping to understand a new vision of man and his fate, the poet saw something so profound, and yet so far beyond the horizon of his world, that he gave it expression in a few brief verses, only to draw back from it at once.

Interestingly enough, the *Odyssey* also has a considerable revival of the older elements of belief that had been so rigorously excluded from the *Iliad*. The eleventh book, the scene in Hades, is filled with ghosts and dark blood and eerie noises, like a canvas of Hieronymus Bosch or Matthias Grünewald, not at all heroic in its texture. In the end, it remained for a poet who stood outside the heroic world to take the great next step. In the case of Hesiod we are certain, as we cannot be for the poet of the *Iliad:* it was he who organized the individual gods into a systematic theogony and made justice into the central problem of existence, human as well as divine. From Hesiod a straight line leads to Aeschylus and the other great tragedians.

In those succeeding centuries the miracle that was Greece unfolded. Homer having made the gods into men, man learned to know himself.

ACKNOWLEDGMENTS

BIBLIOGRAPHICAL ESSAY

SOURCE REFERENCES

INDEXES

Acknowledgments

I am indebted to Professor Karl Polanyi of Columbia University for many stimulating discussions about the comparative study of institutions and for his always interesting and valuable suggestions; to Professors C. M. Arensberg and Martin Ostwald of Columbia, Professor Friedrich Solmsen of Cornell, Dr. Herbert Marcuse of Harvard, and N. M. Halper, all of whom also read the manuscript of this book and offered much wise counsel.

Translations of Hesiod and the Homeric Hymns, by H. G. Evelyn-White, have been reprinted from the Loeb Classical Library by permission of the publishers, Harvard University Press, Cambridge, Massachusetts.

To Pascal Covici of The Viking Press I owe a special debt of gratitude for his personal interest in my work and for much helpful encouragement.

——— M. I. F.

Englewood, New Jersey
April 1954

Bibliographical Essay

∿∿∿∿∿∿∿∿∿∿∿∿∿∿∿∿∿∿∿∿∿∿∿∿∿∿∿∿∿∿∿∿∿

Year after year Homer is the subject of a staggering number of publications. The most recent issue of *L'Année philologique* (Paris: Les Belles Lettres), the invaluable bibliographical guide to Greek and Roman studies, lists 13 books and 61 articles about Homer for the single year 1951 (in addition to editions, translations, or special chapters on Homer in books of greater scope). Of these, 23 are in English, 23 in German, 11 in French, and the remainder in Dutch, Greek, Italian, Latin, or Spanish.

The aim of the following pages is to suggest where the reader may find more extensive discussions of various points raised in this book as well as alternative interpretations. The emphasis is on the most recent publications, many of which have bibliographies of the older literature. With some unavoidable exceptions, only works in English have been noted, and among those, only books which require no knowledge of Greek and no expert acquaintance with Greek history and its modern scholarship. The second limitation will explain the absence of many important studies, such as Friedrich Solmsen, *Hesiod and Aeschylus* (Ithaca: Cornell University Press, 1949), or H. T. Wade-Gery, *The Poet of the Iliad* (Cambridge University Press, 1952).

HOMER AND HISTORY

Every history of Greece attempts to place the world of the Homeric poems in its relationship both with the older, so-called Aegean civilization and with the later history of the Hellenes. It is unneces-

158The World of Odysseus

sary to cite such works by name, except to call attention to the chapters on early Greece in *The Cambridge Ancient History,* volume 3 (Cambridge University Press, 1925). Thomas Day Seymour, *Life in the Homeric Age* (New York: Macmillan, 1907), a massive work of 700 pages, is stronger on what was once generally known as "antiquities"—dress, animals, furniture, and the like—than on institutions. It is not altogether trustworthy in its reporting and it needs much correction as the result of a half century of archaeological discovery. The shorter work of A. G. Keller, *Homeric Society* (New York: Longmans Green, 1902), though written by a trained student of social institutions who does not try, like Seymour, to make a genteel poet of Homer, is rigidly bound to certain theories of social evolution which few scholars will find acceptable today.

M. Cary, *The Geographic Background of Greek and Roman History* (Oxford: Clarendon, 1949); Sir Frederic George Kenyon, *Books and Readers in Ancient Greece and Rome* (2d edition, Oxford: Clarendon, 1951); and H. J. Rose, *A Handbook of Greek Mythology* (5th edition, London: Methuen, 1953), are the best introductions in English to their respective subjects. For an examination of the various theories about the nature of myth and its relationship to ritual, see Clyde Kluckhohn, "Myths and Rituals: A General Theory," in *Harvard Theological Review,* volume 35 (1942), 45–79.

C. M. Bowra, *Heroic Poetry* (London: Macmillan, 1952) is the most comprehensive study of heroic poetry as a genre, with rich illustrative material from all over the world. For an excellent introduction to the historical problem of the Homeric poems and their composition, see Rhys Carpenter, *Folk Tale, Fiction and Saga in the Homeric Epics* (University of California Press, 1946), especially Chapters 1–5. For an altogether different conception, rooted in Jungian psychology, of the hero of myth and legend, see Joseph Campbell, *The Hero with a Thousand Faces* (New York: Pantheon, 1949): "The symbols of mythology . . . are spontaneous productions of the psyche, and each bears within it, undamaged, the germ power of its source" (p. 4). In *Hermathena,* a journal published by Trinity College, Dublin, a series of articles by W. B. Stanford, "Studies in the Characterization of Ulysses," examines the remarkably varied images of Odysseus from antiquity to our own day; the first article appeared in No. 73 (May 1949).

H. L. Lorimer, *Homer and the Monuments* (London: Macmillan, 1950), is an exhaustive study of all the archaeological evidence even remotely relevant to the Homeric poems. It is a book entirely for the specialist; others will probably profit more from Martin P. Nilsson, *Homer and Mycenae* (London: Methuen, 1933). Nilsson has long been the strongest proponent of the view that the Homeric poems reflect the Mycenaean world in essentials, in which he is joined by George Thomson, *Studies in Ancient Greek Society: The Prehistoric Aegean* (New York: International Publishers, 1949). The latter, the most systematic orthodox Marxist analysis in English ("orthodox" in the specific sense that it rests on the anthropology of Morgan and Engels), holds firmly to the position (shared by some non-Marxist scholars) that matriarchy had been the prevailing principle of social organization in the second millennium B.C., and that traces of it are clearly evidenced in Homer. On Schliemann's work, Stanley Casson, *The Discovery of Man* (New York: Harper, 1939), Chapter 5, though brief, is better than either the breathless enthusiasm of C. W. Ceram, *Gods, Graves, and Scholars*, translated by E. B. Garside (New York: Knopf, 1951), Chapters 4–5, or Emil Ludwig's characteristically imaginative biography, *Schliemann of Troy,* translated by D. F. Tait (Boston: Little, Brown, 1931).

INSTITUTIONS

The only modern attempts at a systematic account of the Homeric economy are Gustave Glotz, *Ancient Greece at Work,* translated by M. R. Dobie (New York: Knopf, 1926), Part I, which takes a different view on essential points from the ones expressed in this book; and, more briefly, Johannes Hasebroek, *Griechische Wirtschafts- und Gesellschaftsgeschichte bis zur Perserzeit* (Tübingen: Mohr, 1931), Chapters 1–2, with which the present volume is in closer agreement. On the Phoenicians and other peoples who impinged on the world of Odysseus, and their economic relations, see F. M. Heichelheim, *Wirtschaftsgeschichte des Altertums,* volume 1 (Leiden: Sijthoff, 1938), Chapter 5, to be issued in a revised and enlarged English version by the same publisher during 1954.

By far the best studies of labor are two articles by André Aymard, "L'Idée de travail dans la Grèce archaïque," in *Journal de psychologie,* volume 41 (1948), pp. 29–45; and "Hiérarchie du travail et autarcie individuelle dans la Grèce archaïque," in *Revue d'histoire de la philosophie et d'histoire générale de la civilisation,* volume 11 (1943), pp. 124–46. I know of no serious discussion of the role of gifts in the world of Odysseus, and there seems to be no systematic account in English of gift-giving in primitive and archaic society generally. Melville J. Herskovits, *Economic Anthropology* (New York: Knopf, 1952), Chapter 8, is too narrow and therefore incomplete, although it provides a considerable bibliography of materials in anthropological field studies. One must still go back to the pioneering study—unfortunately a fragment of unusual difficulty—of Marcel Mauss, "Essai sur le don," in his *Sociologie et anthropologie* (Paris: P.U.F., 1950), pp. 143–279, originally published in *L'Année sociologique* for 1923/24.

The best introduction to kinship and community is Gustave Glotz, *The Greek City and Its Institutions,* translated by N. Mallinson (New York: Knopf, 1930; Barnes and Noble, 1950), pp. 1–60. Under the influence of Fustel de Coulanges, Glotz tended to see a linear evolution from clan to state and therefore to ignore the significance of the *oikos,* which had a family at its core but which was not a kinship institution in the proper sense. This is clear from the tripartite division of his classic six-hundred-page study, *La Solidarité de la famille dans le droit criminel en Grèce* (Paris: Fontemoing, 1904): 1. The sovereign family, 2. The city against the family, 3. The sovereign city.

MAN AND THE GODS

There could be no better way to begin a study of the Homeric image of man and his gods than by reading in two recent complementary books: Bruno Snell, *The Discovery of the Mind,* translated by T. G. Rosenmeyer (Cambridge: Harvard University Press, 1953), especially Chapters 1, 2, and 8; and E. R. Dodds, *The Greeks and the Irrational* (University of California Press, 1951), especially Chapters 1–3. Erland Ehnmark, *The Idea of God in Homer* (Uppsala: Almqvist & Wiksell, 1935), provides an especially clear, systematic analysis of the conception of divinity (as distinct from the myths about the individual gods). On the place of Homeric religion within the general history of Greek religion, see the first half of Martin P. Nilsson, *A History of Greek Religion,* translated by F. J. Fielden (2nd edition, Oxford: Clarendon, 1949)—the point should be repeated that Nilsson here, as in all his writings, represents the extreme "pro-Mycenaean" position—and the still valuable, though now somewhat out-of-fashion, book by Gilbert Murray, *The Rise of the Greek Epic* (3d edition, Oxford: Clarendon, 1924), a work which also has much of interest to say about other aspects of the poems.

A recent brief paper by Hermann Strasburger, "Der soziologische Aspekt der Homerischen Epen," in *Gymnasium,* volume 60 (1953), pp. 97–114, argues that the quality of the Homeric heroes was essentially "peasant" in nature. Although the categories of Strasburger's analysis are dubious, the article is most suggestive and filled with insights. In flat opposition, Werner Jaeger, *Paideia: The Ideals of Greek Culture,* translated by Gilbert Highet, volume 1 (Oxford: Blackwell, 1939), Chapters 1–3, insists that the two poems, and the *Odyssey* in particular, were consciously designed as educational instruments, as it were, for the cultivation of aristocratic ideals (which Jaeger conceives to be universally valid for mankind and necessary for the survival of civilization).

A NOTE ON TRANSLATIONS OF HOMER

For the student who is immediately concerned with Homer as a source of historical information, the literary merits of a translation must take second place to its literalness. The greater a translation is as a work of art, the less likely is it to retain the precision the historian desires in what we may call the technical words and phrases. This rule, generally valid for all poetry, is all the more so in the case of Homer because, despite more than a century of the most intensive philological study, the fact still remains that the "uncertainty of word-meanings in Homer extends very far," particularly with the many words, usually adjectives, whose sole function is to give coloring and overtones to the underlying narrative. (Manu Leumann, *Homerische Wörter*. Basel: Reinhardt, 1950, p. 2.)

In the judgments which follow, therefore, the concern is solely with the usefulness of a translation for historical study, and not with aesthetic considerations. The main test, apart from the obvious one of general accuracy, is in the care with which words meaning "treasure," "guest-friend," "god-equal," and the like, are rendered, even at the expense of euphony or at the risk of monotony. That test rules out all verse translations, although Richmond Lattimore's *Iliad* (University of Chicago Press, 1951) comes very near to being an exception; and translations which seek a modern colloquial Homer, in particular the versions of the two poems by E. V. Rieu (Penguin Books) and that of the *Odyssey* by T. E. Shaw (New York: Oxford University Press, 1932).

On the whole, the most faithful translations are the *Iliad* of Andrew Lang, Walter Leaf, and Ernest Myers, and the *Odyssey* by Lang and S. H. Butcher (both available in various editions), to which all subsequent English prose versions are heavily indebted. "I very readily admit," wrote Samuel Butler in the preface to his own *Iliad*, "that Dr. Leaf has in the main kept more closely to the words of Homer." The chief weaknesses in the work of Leaf and his colleagues are an excessive archaism (e.g., "thrall," "maugre," "meed of honor") and a practice on some occasions of expanding the text slightly, for clarification, without any indication that interpolations have been made. The Loeb Classical Library *Iliad* and *Odyssey,* by A. T. Murray, largely eliminate both those weaknesses, but seem a little less precise. The only other translations on the same level of accuracy are the *Iliad* of A. H. Chase and W. G. Perry, Jr. (Boston: Little, Brown, 1950), which unfortunately does not indicate the line numbers and is therefore not convenient for reference purposes; and the *Odyssey* of George H. Palmer, available in several editions (some with expurgations).

Source References

CHAPTER I

Homer and the Greeks

1. *Republic* 606E.
2. *Odyssey* 19.172–77.
3. J. H. Breasted, *Ancient Records of Egypt,* vol. 3 (Chicago: University of Chicago Press, 1906), § 588.
4. *Republic* 607A.
5. Fragment 11, Diels-Kranz edition.
6. Ernst Cassirer, *An Essay on Man* (New York: Anchor Books, 1953), p. 101.
7. Bronislaw Malinowski, "Myth in Primitive Psychology," reprinted in his *Magic, Science and Religion and Other Essays* (New York: Anchor Books, 1954), pp. 100–101.
8. Herodotus 2.45.
9. Cassirer, *An Essay on Man,* p. 21 (the phrasing is his, not Socrates').

CHAPTER II

Bards and Heroes

1. *Works and Days* 156–73 (translated by H. G. Evelyn-White in the Loeb Classical Library).
2. *Odyssey* 1.272.
3. Rhys Carpenter, *Folk Tale, Fiction and Saga in the Homeric Epics* (Berkeley: University of California Press, 1946), p. 165.
4. *Odyssey* 17.382–85.
5. *Iliad* 2.557–58.
6. Diogenes, *Lives* 1.57.

7. *Phaedrus* 252B.
8. Translated by H. G. Evelyn-White in the Loeb Classical Library.
9. See Thucydides 3.104.4.
10. *Iliad* 1.70.
11. *Odyssey* 22.347–48.
12. *Odyssey* 8.44.
13. *Odyssey* 8.487–91.
14. *Odyssey* 8.79.
15. Quoted from C. M. Bowra, *Heroic Poetry* (London: The Macmillan Company, 1952), p. 41.
16. Ibid., p. 40.
17. Carpenter, *Folk Tale, Fiction and Saga*, p. 51.
18. Euripides, *Helen* 108.
19. Herodotus 1.4.
20. *Iliad* 11.670–84.
21. Carpenter, *Folk Tale, Fiction and Saga*, p. 32.
22. Bowra, *Heroic Poetry*, p. 132.
23. *Poetics* 24.13.
24. *Table Talk*, May 12, 1830.

CHAPTER III

Wealth and Labor

1. *Iliad* 2.488–89.
2. *Odyssey* 14.98–99.
3. *Odyssey* 2.123.
4. *Iliad* 6.450–58.
5. *Odyssey* 1.430–33.
6. Carleton S. Coon, *Caravan: The Story of the Middle East* (New York: Henry Holt and Company, 1951), p. 305.
7. *Odyssey* 3.425–38.
8. *Iliad* 23.833–35.
9. *Odyssey* 18.346–61.
10. *Iliad* 21.441–52.
11. *Odyssey* 11.489–91.
12. *Iliad* 23.90.
13. *Odyssey* 4.22–23.
14. *Odyssey* 14.199–212.
15. *Odyssey* 9.108.
16. *Odyssey* 4.590–605.
17. *Odyssey* 2.337–42.
18. *Odyssey* 9.39–42. The final line also appears in the *Iliad*, 11.705.
19. Bronislaw Malinowski, *Crime and Custom in Savage Society* (New York: Humanities Press, 1952), p. 40.
20. *Odyssey* 24.274–85.
21. *Odyssey* 1.311–18.

22. Marc Bloch, in *The Cambridge Economic History,* ed. by J. H. Clapham and Eileen Power, vol. 1 (Cambridge, England: Cambridge University Press, 1941), p. 262. Bloch is discussing the early Germanic world described by Tacitus.
23. *Iliad* 6.234–36.
24. *Odyssey* 15.536–38, 17.163–65, 19.309–11.
25. *Odyssey* 4.649–51.
26. *Odyssey* 1.430–31.
27. *Iliad* 9.328–31.
28. *Laws* 941B.
29. *Odyssey* 8.145–64.
30. *Odyssey* 19.395–97.
31. *Philoctetes* 407–408.
32. *Odyssey* 15.415–16.
33. Aristotle, *Rhetoric* 1.9, 1367a32, writing with specific reference to labor.
34. *Iliad* 18.410–15.
35. *Iliad* 1.599–600.
36. *Odyssey* 6.232–34.

CHAPTER IV

Household, Kin, and Community

1. *Odyssey* 1.296–97.
2. *Odyssey* 24.433–35.
3. *Odyssey* 2.42–46.
4. *Odyssey* 2.1–8.
5. *Iliad* 1.22–25, 376–79.
6. *Iliad* 1.304–305.
7. *Iliad* 9.100.
8. e.g., *Iliad* 2.669.
9. *Iliad* 6.478.
10. *Odyssey* 1.394–96.
11. *Odyssey* 1.386–402.
12. *Odyssey* 20.336–37.
13. *Odyssey* 2.246–51.
14. *Odyssey* 13.383–85.
15. *Iliad* 20.179–83.
16. *Odyssey* 11.494–503.
17. *Odyssey* 1.356–59, 21.350–53.
18. *Odyssey* 1.275–78.
19. *Odyssey* 2.132–33.
20. *Odyssey* 20.341–44.
21. *Odyssey* 15.16–18.
22. *Odyssey* 7.73–74.
23. *Odyssey* 6.313–15; repeated by Athena, 7.75–77.
24. *Odyssey* 11.338.

25. *Odyssey* 11.346.
26. *Odyssey* 6.196–97.
27. *Odyssey* 1.245–47, repeated 16.122–24; with variations, 19.130–32.
28. *Odyssey* 2.52–54.
29. *Odyssey* 2.239–41.
30. *Odyssey* 24.413.
31. *Odyssey* 23.117–22.
32. *Odyssey* 2.244–45.
33. *Odyssey* 2.250–51.
34. *Odyssey* 16.375–82.
35. *Odyssey* 16.425–27.
36. *Odyssey* 3.214–15.
37. *Odyssey* 16.95–96.
38. *Odyssey* 3.193–98.
39. *Odyssey* 1.392–93.
40. *Odyssey* 14.230–33.
41. *Iliad* 1.165–68.
42. *Odyssey* 13.13–15.
43. Quoted from Hermann Fränkel, *Die Homerischen Gleichnisse* (Göttingen: Vandenhoeck, 1921), p. 60.
44. *Iliad* 12.310–21.
45. *Odyssey* 19.107–14.
46. *Iliad* 6.119–231.
47. Herodotus 1.69.
48. *Odyssey* 6.201–205.
49. *Odyssey* 7.31–32.
50. *Odyssey* 9.370.
51. *Odyssey* 9.275–76.
52. *Odyssey* 14.57–58.
53. *Odyssey* 8.557–59.
54. *Odyssey* 24.283.
55. *Iliad* 24.397–400.
56. *Odyssey* 15.324.
57. *Iliad* 13.295, 304.
58. A. R. Radcliffe-Brown, *Structure and Function in Primitive Society* (London: Cohen & West, 1952), p. 29.
59. *Iliad* 2.188–202.

CHAPTER V

Morals and Values

1. *Iliad* 23.259–61.
2. *Iliad* 23.542–85.
3. *Iliad* 2.211–78.
4. *Iliad* 9.443.
5. *Odyssey* 13.295.

6. *Iliad* 1.258.
7. *Iliad* 22.105–107, 124–25.
8. *Iliad* 12.243.
9. Bruno Snell, *The Discovery of the Mind,* translated by T. G. Rosenmeyer (Cambridge, Mass.: Harvard University Press, 1953), p. 160.
10. *Iliad* 9.121–56.
11. *Iliad* 9.632–38.
12. *The Theory of the Leisure Class,* in *The Portable Veblen,* edited by Max Lerner (New York: The Viking Press, 1948), p. 69.
13. *Iliad* 11.145–47.
14. *Homer's Contest,* in *The Portable Nietzsche,* translated and edited by Walter Kaufmann (New York: The Viking Press, 1954), p. 32.
15. *Iliad* 23.510–13.
16. *Odyssey* 4.613–18, repeated 15.113–18.
17. *Odyssey* 19.272–84.
18. *Odyssey* 19.203.
19. *Odyssey* 11.358–61.
20. *Iliad* 1.152–54.
21. *Iliad* 9.406–407.
22. *Iliad* 1.212–14.
23. *Odyssey* 9.5–10.
24. *Iliad* 4.257–60.
25. *Odyssey* 1.374–75, repeated 2.139–40.
26. *Iliad* 24.801–804.
27. *Iliad* 9.70.
28. *Odyssey* 14.45–47.
29. *Odyssey* 14.432–46.
30. *Iliad* 22.492–98.
31. A. T. Murray, in the Loeb Classical Library (*Iliad* 9.340–41). Lang, Leaf, and Myers reads: "Do then the sons of Atreus alone of mortal men love their wives?"
32. *Iliad* 1.113–14.
33. *Odyssey* 10.14.
34. *Odyssey* 6.314–15; repeated by Athena, 7.76–77, and used earlier by Zeus, 5.41–42, and by Hermes, 5.114–15.
35. *Odyssey* 8.317–20.
36. *Odyssey* 16.17–18.
37. Gilbert Murray, *The Rise of the Greek Epic* (3d ed., Oxford: The Clarendon Press, 1924), p. 125.
38. *Nicomachean Ethics* 8.7.1–2.
39. *Iliad* 3.351–54.
40. *Odyssey* 15.20–23.
41. *Iliad* 3.380–415.
42. *Iliad* 3.139–40.
43. *Odyssey* 23.11–14.
44. *Odyssey* 13.130.

45. *Odyssey* 5.118–20.
46. *Iliad* 15.187–93.
47. *Iliad* 15.184–86.
48. *Iliad* 8.209–11.
49. *Iliad* 5.331.
50. *Iliad* 5.428–30.
51. *Iliad* 1.533–34.
52. *Odyssey* 1.68–79.
53. *Iliad* 23.175–76.
54. *Odyssey* 13.291–99.
55. *Iliad* 24.527–33.
56. E. R. Dodds, *The Greeks and the Irrational* (Berkeley and Los Angeles: University of California Press, 1951), p. 29.
57. Hesiod, *Works and Days* 176–78.
58. Dodds, *The Greeks and the Irrational*, p. 76.
59. *Odyssey* 24.351–52.
60. *Iliad* 4.44–54.
61. *Odyssey* 22.408–13.

Index of Passages Quoted

(NOTE: *All the translations quoted in the text are the author's, except the quotations from Hesiod and the Hymn to Apollo. Italic figures indicate pages in this book; figures in parentheses indicate reference numbers following quotations.*)

95–96, 97 (37)
122–24, *93* (27)
375–82, *96* (34)
425–27, *97* (35)
Book 17:163–65, *64* (24)
382–85, *30, 51* (4)
Book 18:346–61, *53* (9)
Book 19:107–14, *101–102* (45)
130–32, *93* (27)
172–77, *5–6* (2)
203, *131* (18)
272–84, *131* (17)
309–11, *64* (24)
395–97, *68* (30)
Book 20:336–37, *87* (12)
341–44, *91* (20)
Book 21:350–53, *91* (17)
Book 22:347–48, *36* (11)
408–13, *153* (61)
Book 23:11–14, *141* (43)
117–22, *95* (31)
Book 24:109–13, *103*
115–19, *108*
205–10, *90*
274–85, *62* (20)
283, *108* (54)
351–52, *152* (59)
413, *95* (30)
433–35, *78* (2)
ARISTOTLE
Nicomachean Ethics 8:7.1–2, *139* (38)

Poetics 24.13, *43* (23)
Rhetoric 1.9,1367a32, *70–71* (33)
DIOGENES LAERTIUS
Lives of the Philosophers
1.57, *31* (6)
3.41–43, *59*
EURIPIDES
Helen 108, *39* (18)
HERODOTUS
1.4, *40–41* (19)
1.69, *105* (47)
2.45, *13* (8)
HESIOD
Theogony 22–34, *35*
Works and Days
156–73, *17–18* (1)
159–60, *147*
176–78, *151* (57)
HYMN TO APOLLO
166–76, *34*
PLATO
Laws 941B, *67* (28)
Phaedrus 252B, *33* (7)
Republic
606E, *3* (1)
607A, *11* (4)
SOPHOCLES
Philoctetes 407–408, *68* (31)
THUCYDIDES
3.104.4, *34* (9)
XENOPHANES
fragment 11, *11* (5)

General Index

Achaeans, 6–7
Achchiyava, 6–7, 40
Achilles: epithets for, 21; as hero, 24, 121, 123, 125–26, 131–32, 148–49; and Patroclus, 55, 114, 126, 137–38, 148–49
Aeneid, see Vergil
Aeolic, 8
Agamemnon: status and character of, 76, 123
Ages of man, 17–19; *see also* Hero, age of heroes
Agora, see Assembly
Agriculture, 53, 57
Alcinous, *see* Phaeacia
Alexander, *see* Paris
Alexandria, *see* Egypt, Greek literature in
Alphabet, 8–9
Anassein, 85
Anthropomorphism, *see under* Gods
Aphrodite: and Helen, 139, 141; power of, 144, 146
Apollo: and Dionysus, 151; and prophecy, 36; and the Trojans, 53–54, 82
Arbitration, 115–17
Arete (queen of the Phaeacians), 92–93, 139
Argives, 6

Aristocracy, *see* Nobility
Aristotle on Homer, 43
Arms and armor, 36, 39–40
Army, 46–47, 108–109; and assembly, 81–83; *see also* War
Assembly, 20, 79–84, 94–96, 115–116, 118–19; *see also* Counsel
Atarshiyash, 6
Athena: characterization of, 21, 140, 149–50; and craftsmanship, 72; and Odysseus, 24, 47, 53, 69, 105–106, 149–50; and Telemachus, 76–79, 91–92
Athens and Homer, 30–32

Bard: divine inspiration of, 34–36; in Homer, 30, 36, 49, 51, 52; among the Slavs, 21–22, 33; *see also* Heroic poetry; Rhapsodist
Basileus, 84, 86, 145; *see also* Kingship
Blood-feud, 24, 77–78, 95–99, 117, 126, 160
Booty: distribution of, 61, 66, 82, 99–100; nature of, 41, 49–50, 52, 59, 99; as source of supplies, 59, 61, 99–100; as trophy of heroic behavior, 19–20, 41, 82, 125–28, 130

Bravery, *see* Prowess
Bronze, *see* Metal
Burial, *see* Funeral

Cattle, *see* Money; Pasturage
Chariots, 39–40, 114
Child and parent, 135–37
Commoners, 49, 51–56, 70–71, 83–84; attitudes and values of, 118–121; and kingship, 94–97, 100–103; and political power, 113, 118–19, 125; and religion, 151
Community, 79–81, 84–85, 105, 109–13, 117, 124–25, 129, 160
Competition and contest, 126–29; *see also* Games
Counsel, 121–25, 145, 149–50; *see also* Public opinion
Courage; *see* Prowess
Craftsmen, 30, 33, 51–52, 71–72; *see also* Hephaestus
Crime and criminal law; *see* Blood-feud
Cruelty, 127–28, 148–49
Custom, 66, 111
Cyclopes, 57, 79, 106

Danaans, 6
Demeter, 148, 151
Demi-gods, 17, 147
Demioergoi, 30, 51–52; *see also* Craftsmen
Demos, see Commoners
Dionysus, 151
Distribution of goods, 59–60, 63, 66; *see also* Gifts; Trade
Divorce, 137
Dmos, 55
Doulos, 55
Dowry, *see* Marriage and gifts
Drester, 49

Egypt: Achaean raid on, 7; Greek literature in, 10–11, 27, 31
Elders, council of, 83–84, 134; *see also* Counsel

Ethics, *see* Morals
Exchange, *see* Gifts; Trade
Exile, 57, 95, 126

Family, 60, 78, 137; *see also* Household; Kinship
Fate, 145, 150
Feasting, 92, 106, 133–36
Festivals, *see* Games
Feud, *see* Blood-feud
Foreign affairs, 101, 103–106; *see also* War
Foreigners: as craftsmen, 30, 34, 52; hostility to, 105–108; sharing meal with, 134–35
Friendship; *see* Guest-friendship; Love
Funeral and burial, 39, 126, 134, 148–49; games, 27, 114–16, 128

Games, 27, 29–30, 52, 68–69, 114–116, 128
Gifts, 58–59, 61–65, 100–103, 129–130, 132–33, 148, 160; as amends, 64, 125–26, 150; and marriage, 64, 91–94
Gods: as ancestors of men, 56, 142; anthropomorphism, 143–47; and bards, 34–36; fear and love of, 150–51; and feasts, 135; and festivals, 29; and gifts, 63, 100–101, 119, 148, 150; and goddesses, 140; intervention of, 24–25, 48–49, 141–45; and justice, 101–102, 116, 139–40, 150–54; of nature, 147–148; and *themis*, 79, 106–107; and work, 71–72; *see also* Magic; Myth; Prayer; Religion; Sacrifice; Temples; *and* names of individual gods
Gold; *see* Metal; Treasure
Greeks: geographic spread of, 4–5, 14, 25; names for, 6–7; political organization of, 14, 26–27; prehistory of, 4–9, 16, 80; *see also* Language; Literature; Writing

Guest-friendship, 63, 92, 103–109, 133

Hades, 54, 90, 103, 121, 143, 145, 153
Hector: as Greek name, 38; as hero, 89, 121, 124–25; Theban myth of, 38
Helen, 139–41
Helius, 147–48
Hellenes; *see* Greeks
Hephaestus: as craftsman, 71–72, 119, 130
Hera, character of, 140, 144, 152
Heracles, 13–14
Herald, 51, 52, 81–82, 115, 120
Hermes, 68–69
Hero: age of heroes, 17–20; nature of, 19–20, 25, 75–76; *see also* Honor; Prowess; Status and values; *and* names of individual heroes
Heroic poetry, 21–23, 158; repetition (formulas) in, 21–23, 40, 85; *see also* Bard; Homer and history; *Iliad; Odyssey*
Hesiod, 4, 24, 26, 35–36, 120; and the age of heroes, 17–19; and the gods, 35–36, 102, 147, 153–54; Greek attitudes to, 11
Hissarlik, 37–38
Hittites, 6–8
Homer: and the development of Greek religion, 11, 146–54; and the Greeks, 3–4, 11, 29–36, 67, 161; and history, 12–14, 18–19, 25–45, 67, 77, 88, 112, 119–20, 157–59; identity of, 4, 19, 23–24, 26–27, 33–34, 36; language of, 8, 23, 32 (*see also* Heroic poetry, repetition in); and myth, 11–12, 15–16, 27, 77, 112; popularity of, 11, 28, 32; view of man in, 15–16, 20, 121, 141–43, 146–47, 161; *see also Iliad; Odyssey*
Homeric Hymns, 33–34
Homerids, 33–34

Homosexuality, 137–38
Honor, 19–20, 114–18, 121–32, 144
Hospitality, *see* Feasts; Foreigners; Guest-friendship
Household, 52–61, 69, 85–87, 98–99, 109–12; *see also* Family

Ichor, 146, 147
Iliad: compared with *Odyssey*, 24, 151–54; composition and structure of, 4, 21, 23, 27–29; English translations of, 162–63; interpolations in, 30–31, 44; textual history of, 27, 30–34; theme of, 82, 125–126
Ilion, *see* Troy
Inheritance, 56; *see also* Kingship and succession
Ionian, 6, 8, 29
Iron, *see* Metal
Italy, 25–26
Ithaca, topography of, in the *Odyssey*, 26

Justice, 13, 25, 101–102, 150–54; judicial procedure, 115–17, 120

Keimelion, 58
Kingship, 47–48, 109; and assembly, 81–84; and commoners, 94–97, 100–103; and gift-giving, 100–103, 133; and power, 83–100, 112–13, 117, 123, 144; and royal wealth, 99–101, 130–31; and succession, 85–98, 143
Kinship, 77–78, 85, 110–11, 125, 135–36, 160; and blood-feud, 77–78; *see also* Family

Labor, *see* Work
Laertes: and kingship in Ithaca, 89–90
Land, 57, 99
Language: Greek, 4–5, 8–9; Indo-European, 8; *see also* Homer, language of

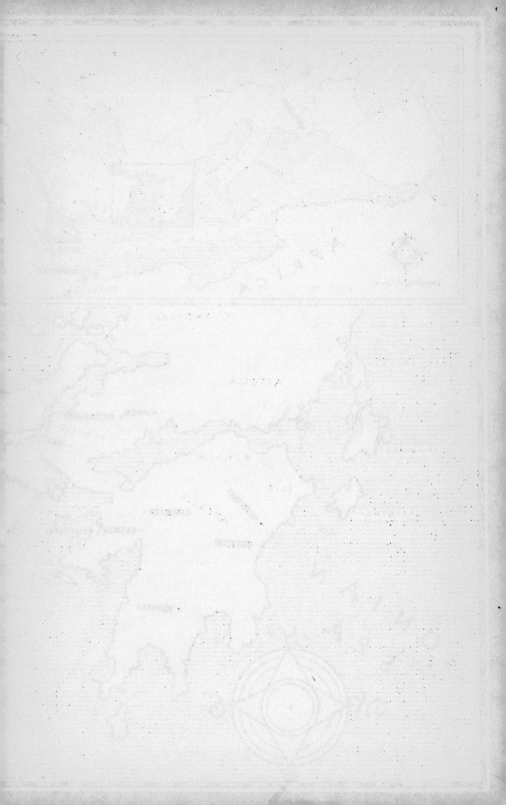

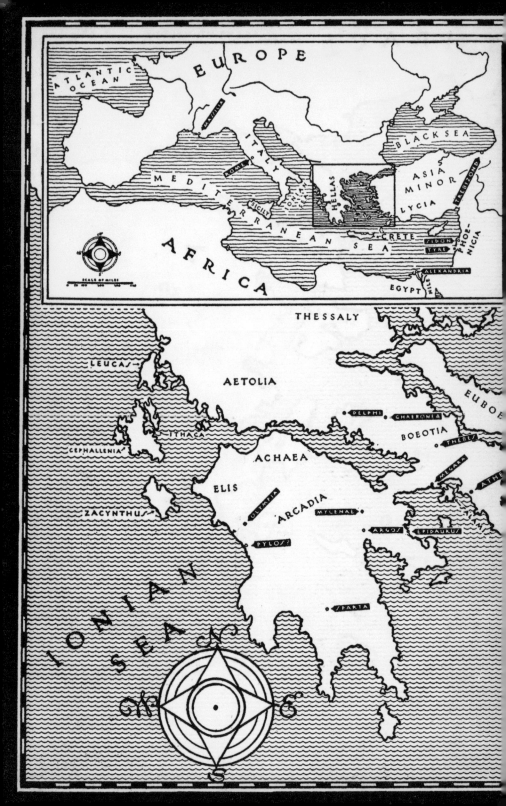